Southern antiques & folk art

by Robert Morton

design
by Ladislav Svatos

Oxmoor House, Inc.

Birmingham

SOUTHERN ANTIQUES & FOLK ART

ISBN 0-8487-0420-7
Library of Congress Catalog Card Number: 76-14114
Printed in the United States of America
Copyright © 1976 by Oxmoor House, Inc.
P. O. Box 2463, Birmingham, Alabama 35243
All rights reserved
First Edition

Oxmoor House, Inc., is the Book Division
of The Progressive Farmer Company:
Eugene Butler *Chairman of the Board and Editor-in-Chief*
Emory Cunningham *President and Publisher*
Vernon Owens, Jr. *Senior Executive Vice President*
Roger McGuire *Executive Vice President*
Leslie B. Adams, Jr. *Vice President and Director of Book Division*

Southern Antiques & Folk Art was developed jointly by
Oxmoor House, Inc., and Media Projects, Inc.
Publication under the direction of:
John Logue *Editor-in-Chief*
Karen Phillips *Editor*
Robert L. Nance *Production Manager*
Harry Lerner *Graphic Arts Consultant*

Project management by Media Projects, Inc.,
under the direction of:
Carter Smith, Jr. *President*
Edith Alston *Project Editor*

Photography by
Lee Boltin, Taylor Lewis, Brad Rauschenberg

Title page: John F. Amelung of Frederick, Maryland made this amethyst-colored glass sugar bowl about 1790. *Right:* A mahogany lady's writing cabinet from Baltimore.

The publishers
gratefully acknowledge the invaluable assistance
tendered in the preparation of this book by
our Editorial Advisory Board:

Gray D. Boone,
Publisher and Editor, ANTIQUE MONTHLY,
Tuscaloosa, Alabama

Graham Hood,
Director of Collections, Colonial Williamsburg, Inc.,
Williamsburg, Virginia

Charlotte Hooker,
President, Houston Antique Museum,
Chattanooga, Tennessee

Frank L. Horton,
Director, Museum of Early Southern Decorative Arts,
Winston-Salem, North Carolina

Lonn Taylor,
Director, Winedale Inn – A Museum of Cultural History,
University of Texas at Austin

Mary Victor,
Director, Fine Arts Museum of the South
at Mobile, Alabama

Contents

An introduction. Nearly thirty years ago, at a forum on American antiques, one of the speakers – a distinguished scholar and curator of the decorative arts – remarked that "little of artistic merit was made south of Baltimore." No one took exception. Whereupon a southern lady rose to inquire whether he had made his statement out of prejudice – or ignorance. Slightly taken aback, the speaker good-humoredly admitted that he had spoken largely out of ignorance. 🙬 This anecdote invariably draws a smile. But in a profound way, there is nothing funny about it at all. Actually, in 1949, so little was known about southern-made furniture, silver, ceramics, textiles, and folk art, that there was virtually no published literature on them. One inaccurate book, published in 1933, had long been out of print. Even worse, the scholarly view in the many existing books on American antiques – and there were dozens – extended only about as far south as Philadelphia. Southerners themselves were doing little to learn about their own heritage or to correct the narrow view of writers who had suggested that New England antiques were the beginning and the end of the spectrum. 🙬 Therefore, it is hard to blame the forum speaker for his ignorance. But it was clear that if *he* was ignorant, who was knowledgeable? To begin redress of the situation, a major show of southern furniture was organized in Richmond in 1952 as a cooperative venture of Colonial Williamsburg, The Virginia Museum of Fine Arts and The Magazine *Antiques.* It was immediately apparent that the neglected material was rich and varied. It was also evident that

A superb Moravian plate from about 1795.

there was work to be done to bring this aspect of southern culture to light. ❧ Why had the decorative arts in the South been ignored for so long? The question is a tantalizing one for which no easy answers exist. A frequent guess is that the Civil War destroyed much material. In fact, except for the looting of large amounts of silver (much of which was hammered flat, stuffed in barrels, and carted off for its value as pure metal), much finely-crafted furniture, ceramics, and textiles survived. Thus, the war was not a prime destroyer, though of course many houses were burned or damaged by bombardment and some objects were ruined by careless troops billeted in private homes. What was destroyed by the war primarily, however, was the wealth of many families who owned fine things. In essence, the South's social fabric was ripped apart. With its destruction many valuable objects were sold or lost and fell into obscurity. ❧ Since 1952 a great deal has been done to restore southern antiques to their rightful place among America's finest achievements. Tremendous contributions have been made by the Museum of Early Southern Decorative Arts in Winston-Salem (in the superbly restored Moravian village of Old Salem); by Colonial Williamsburg, with its vast restoration; by the Anglo-American Art Museum in Baton Rouge; and by dozens of other museums, historical societies, and restorations. Especially in Baltimore, Charleston, Savannah, Atlanta, New Orleans, Natchez, Mobile, San Antonio, and Houston, the work goes on. This book is the first broad-scale survey published. It could not exist without the pioneering efforts of many individuals and institutions now collecting and studying the South's great heritage. And the scholars have brought to light much evidence that proves it *is* a great heritage. In every area of creativity, from furniture and silver to household ironware, quilts and folk painting, southern craftsmen hold their own in quality and imagination. As much as any region of America, it reflects the cultural and ethnic diversity of its settlers, from the Scottish and Irish who peopled the Piedmont, to Moravian towns in North Carolina, Shaker communities in Kentucky, the French whose influence pervades Louisiana, and the Germans who left their strong imprint in certain areas of Texas. Not to be ignored, either, is the strength of imagery or the quality of craftsmanship contributed by transplanted Africans and the indigenous North American Indian cultures. ❧ Sadly, as this book reveals, little is known of the men and women who made the treasured objects seen here. Except for the silver, few pieces were signed – usually because it was not a customary practice to do so. Also, many objects have become dislocated from their original settings, and historical information about them has been lost. Nevertheless, they can be seen for their intrinsic worth – for design, use of materials, and the stylistic influences they reveal. And, equally important, every object speaks of the way life was lived in the South. ❧ And that is what this book is really about. The decorative arts in particular show how people lived, not only their tastes, but the things they chose to enhance their style of living. For instance, hospitality in the South is legendary. One may find concrete evidence of the fact in the abundance and quality of furniture designed for elegant serving, and the remarkable variety of a uniquely southern form, the cellaret on high legs. Several basic guidelines served in selecting material for this book. First, the geographical range extends from Baltimore to Texas, including the eastern seaboard – Virginia, the Carolinas, Georgia – inland to Kentucky, Tennessee, and Arkansas, down into the Deep South of Alabama, Louisiana and Mississippi. Concerning time, all the objects in the book are truly antique by any standard, though some are as young as the first decade of this century. With furniture, however, we stop in the 1860s, for it was just about then that industrially made articles became prevalent in American homes. In the other arts, we were also guided by the last dates that truly individual, hand-crafted work was done. Finally, and most importantly, we have, with only a few exceptions, included objects exclusively *made* in the South, not simply used in southern homes. Also, we have made it a point to illustrate objects in public collections, so that the reader may go to see the actual articles. A last word should be said about the aim and hope of the book. As indicated earlier, this is the first broad-scale survey of its kind. Clearly, in trying to be comprehensive, we have had to be selective and thus have missed some regional variations, and some fine examples similar to things we do show. But by offering this book as a beginning, we have tried to provide an overview that will stimulate further looking, collecting, and reading.

An unknown Charleston woman created this wreath of wool flowers.

Arts of fine living

A Queen Anne candlestand from North Carolina stands beside a magnificent Charleston easy chair.

From the moment they landed at Jamestown, the Virginia colonists were making articles and utensils of daily life. Within a year, a glass factory had been begun, joiners were turning out simple stools and tables, and potters were fashioning earthenware. But the great lure of the new land proved to be its ability to produce tobacco, and though the crafts developed, farming was the prime business. In the Carolinas, the rice culture and the growing of indigo became established. As their agricultural efforts became profitable, and they could afford finer furnishings, many planters sent to England. Thus, we find that much of the South's high-style furniture – as well as its silver, pewter, glass and porcelain – came from abroad. In 1771, the Charleston planter Peter Manigault, wrote his London broker: "Having at last built myself a good house after having lived sixteen years in a bad one I stand in need of some plate and furniture of which I enclose you a list." And when the articles themselves did not cross the Atlantic, English craftsmen and designs did. Quite naturally, even locally-made pieces were modeled after the latest London modes.   By the middle of the 18th Century, however, southern towns and cities had begun to support their own artisans in fairly large numbers. The sources for our information about these men are court records, city directories which listed tradesmen by occupation, and newspapers. A typical notice of the *South Carolina Gazette* of 11 October 1770 reveals that a John Bartlam had opened a pottery and china manufactory: "He already makes what is called Queen's Ware, equal to any imported. . . ." In the areas away from active ports, however, the interest in London fashions and reliance on them necessarily became diluted. As trading towns developed in the Piedmont region and the thriving Chesapeake area (Annapolis supported numerous silversmiths and cabinetmakers), an increasing number of craftsmen set up shop. In the interior of the country, where overland transportation was difficult and expensive, indigenous styles developed which were usually less dependent on English models, and also less sophisticated than the products preferred on the coast. Local materials – cherry wood, for example, which marks much Kentucky furniture – largely took the place of mahogany and satinwood. Another element that contributed to the increasing number of craftsmen in the South – and the diversity of styles – was the settlement of the Back Country by immigrants of continental European background – Germans and Swiss in particular, as well as Scottish, Welsh and Irish. As the frontier was pushed west, rural communities developed a need for craftsmen. In 1813, the citizens of Glasgow, Kentucky, advertised for "A Chair maker, a wagon-maker and a potter" as well as others, stating that "We believe that men of steadiness in these professions will meet with great encouragement in their line of business by the citizens of the country in general." As the South filled with settlers, artisans in every area of the decorative arts found outlets for their work. Though the region remained essentially rural, and imported goods continued to supply many needs – especially for the wealthy – a body of work was being created that the Southerner of today can look upon with pride. And as scholarly studies of southern antiques begin to fill the gaps in the history of their creation and use, our appreciation of the past will become greatly enriched.

Porcelain made in China bears the crest of the Manigault family from South Carolina.

Craft of the cabinetmaker. The finest southern furniture ranks with the best made anywhere, though it seems to be less plentiful than that produced in the North. Much of it remains in private hands, of course, and so is hidden from view. But research projects like the one being carried out by the Museum of Early Southern Decorative Arts are beginning to bring the furniture to light and classify it. Since few pieces are signed by the maker, and since the histories of most are lost or undocumented, identification is difficult. Even identifying a piece as southern may not be easy. But, fortunately, the woods used in the South to make furniture are very characteristic. Most typical of all is southern yellow pine, quite different from northern white pine. Pine, of course, was seldom used as a primary wood – that is, on the visible surfaces of a piece. Mahogany, walnut, maple and cherry – woods with finer and more beautiful grains – were usually sought as primary woods. But for economy's sake, most cabinetmakers used yellow pine for the basic framework of furniture: in this context it is called a secondary wood. In Gulf and East Coast areas, cypress was a common secondary wood. Thus, in examining a mahogany chest, one might be unable to detect its origins unless close study revealed cypress or yellow pine in the structure – in which case, the piece would almost certainly be southern. In addition to woods, style can be a key to identification. Though English models influence much southern craftsmanship, regional variations, types of carving and inlays, and the general forms of pieces can give vital clues to the place of origin and sometimes to individual makers.

Piedmont furniture of the early 19th Century fills a dining room at the Houston Antique Museum in Chattanooga.

Early furniture. The early styles of the Virginia and Carolina settlements before about 1720 are chiefly characterized by turned decoration. Woodworking craftsmen in those days were turners and joiners. The rounded, spindle forms were shaped by "turning" a length of wood on a hand-powered lathe; a joiner made furniture such as chests and tables with joints of flat planks. The stylistic name for these earliest colonial pieces is Jacobean, for James I, who was King of England at the time the Jamestown colony was settled. Although he ruled less than a quarter of a century, his name is applied to most of the furniture of the whole hundred-year period. By the very end of the 1600s, the English monarchs were William and Mary. Their names are applied to a new and relatively lighter style. There was substantial colonization and building in America during the 17th Century, but not much southern Jacobean or William and Mary furniture is known. Quite naturally, as the colonials became more affluent and built larger homes, they wished to furnish them in the latest modes. Much of the early furniture was discarded or relegated to kitchens and other outbuildings where it was used roughly and eventually destroyed. Among the rare surviving pieces are the press cupboard below and the open-gallery court cupboard at left, seen in Crisscross Hall at the Museum of Early Southern Decorative Arts.

One room and a loft made up the living quarters of a family on the eastern shore of Maryland in about 1725. Small in size and probably furnished with only a few basics – like the pieces shown here – the house nevertheless boasted a cheerful blue and red painted fireplace wall.

Below: Probably the oldest piece of Charleston furniture extant is this gate-leg table of about 1700. It is fashioned of cedar and cypress, local woods used in Charleston until about 1830, when the importation of mahogany from the West Indies became so cheap that even modest households could afford it.

By the middle of the 18th Century, the southern planter was beginning to build a larger house and to enjoy a somewhat more luxurious way of life. *Right:* The fall-front desk and bookcase appeared then as a new form. It indicates not only that the rural family had time for reading but that the farmer's business was active enough for him to require more correspondence and record keeping. The emergence of the daybed, a forerunner of the settee or couch, also suggests greater leisure. *Above:* Another sign of the increasing affluence is the appearance of paintings, especially portraits. These flanking the looking glass are unusual on two counts: done in pastel, an uncommon medium in America at the time, they are by this country's first woman artist, Henrietta Johnston.

The transition from the heavily turned pieces of the Jacobean period to the lighter William and Mary style is documented by the furniture on these pages. *Below, left:* This table looks like it might have been made well back in the 1600s. It was in fact produced in about 1734, probably in Ebenezer, Georgia, where a German religious group called Salzburgers had set up a colony. *Below:* By contrast, the candlestand made roughly at the same time, shows a more refined turning.

Comfort as well as elegance became a consideration in the William and Mary period. *Right:* This armchair, for example, has shaped, flat slats for its back rather than the turned spindles of much Jacobean chair construction – an undeniable concession to comfort. *Far right:* A purely visual nicety enhances the oval-top table; its top is slightly beveled on the under side of the edge – a clear effort to make it appear thinner and thus more elegant.

The Queen Anne period. The style is best characterized by lightness and delicacy, by curving lines and a variety of carved details – in particular the scallop shell and acanthus leaf. For instance, in the parlor at left, the tall Maryland desk and bookcase features an imposing broken scroll pediment and high, arched mirrors. The chair before it, made in the Albemarle area of North Carolina and one of a known pair, shows the distinctive Queen Anne cabriole leg with an acanthus leaf carved at the outcurved knee. The ball-and-claw foot is a late development of the Queen Anne period that carries over into the Chippendale style. Interestingly, both the ball-and-claw foot and the acanthus leaf reveal the influence of foreign (in this case, Chinese and classical Greek) design effects upon basically English styles. The commingling of many different motifs and ideas increasingly attracted American buyers and makers of furniture and other decorative arts. While it is virtually impossible to say what is especially "American" or indeed "southern" about our artisans' use of borrowed elements, they are always distinctive, different, and individual. Along with elegant rooms came a need and a desire for pictures; next to portraiture, prints of all kinds and scenic views proved popular. Before a native school had time to develop, many English artists – usually not of the first rank – came over to try their luck in the colonies. A painter about whom little is known named Thomas Leitch (or Leech) arrived in Charleston in 1773. Within a short time, he had painted a handsome view of the town, *(below)* and the following year he sold prints made from his painting – a common practice.

Perhaps the most interesting thing to look for on early furniture is the personal touch of the cabinetmaker – an innovation of design or style that becomes either a trademark or a charming oddity. *Far left:* The man who made this drop-leaf table – otherwise a standard form – introduced a split knee where the long, curving leg meets the square base of the top. One other example of this unusual style is known; it was made in western South Carolina, but nothing at all is known of the maker. Equally distinctive are the boldly flaring cabriole legs of the table below. The ball-and-claw foot – a design motif derived through English furniture from ancient Chinese sources, in which an eagle's claw clutches a pearl – became common on American furniture in the mid-18th Century and continued in use through the Chippendale period. *Right:* Earlier, a pad foot like that on the unusual six-legged, drop-leaf dining table was prevalent. *Far right:* The eccentric little table features unusually large ball-and-claw feet; they are set beneath slender, tapering legs that splay out slightly from a scalloped apron cut in a cupid's bow.

The dressing table — fitted with small drawers for cosmetics and jewelry — came into use just before the Queen Anne period. *Left:* This is an especially fine piece from Charleston; carved on the knees are fleurs-de-lis, an indication that one of the many French Huguenot immigrants to the city may have been a cabinetmaker — and a skilled one.

Right: Covered with a canopy known as a tester (pronounced teester), this handsome Queen Anne bed is fitted with back and side drapes to block drafts. The crewel embroidery, called "bed furniture" in inventories of the time, was changed to lighter material or removed altogether in summer.

A square table with a diagonal gate-leg fold is also known as a corner or "handkerchief" table. Often used in a bedroom and set up for breakfast, the table could be neatly tucked in a corner after the meal. It was the practice in the 18th Century to keep most furniture pushed against walls, unlike the present fashion of "filling" a room.

The blue and red painted woodwork of the fireplace wall of this congenial dining room comes from a North Carolina house built before 1780. The painted design above the fireplace itself is called a fylfot, an ancient abstraction of the sun's shape similar to the Indian swastika and usually associated with good luck. The basic furnishings include Chippendale chairs from North Carolina and a Queen Anne table from Virginia or North Carolina of a slightly earlier date. Beside the fireplace is a cellaret on legs, one of two distinctively southern forms of furniture – the other being the tall, long serving table called a huntboard.

Why the cellaret on legs should have become so popular in the South is a matter for speculation. Perhaps the taller rooms made desirable by warmer climates encouraged the design, for wine tubs – sometimes lined with tin or lead to hold ice – and square bottle cases were known in the North. But the familiar standing cellaret seems common only below Maryland. Fitted with compartments to hold the tapering green or brown glass gin bottles, cellarets were made and used in the South over a long period, as witnessed by the succession of styles in this gallery: a boldly curvaceous Queen Anne type at right, a modest Chippendale version above and an exuberantly decorated country model below.

In Chippendale's style. Thomas Chippendale was one of the first great English cabinetmaker/designers to influence American furniture: not so much through work from his own shop as through his design books – widely circulated in the colonies soon after their first publication in 1754. The handsome library bookcase below is shown with the plate from Chippendale's book which inspired it. But southern craftsmen not only derived information and ideas from Chippendale's drawings, they sometimes combined his designs with other influences. At left is the crowning achievement of an unknown Charleston craftsman. Nearly eleven feet tall, over eight feet wide, and made of mahogany inlaid with ivory and satinwood, the piece shows Chippendale's influence as well as French and Continental inspirations. Its serpentine-front base section with richly grained veneers and its lacy, carved pediment inlaid with flowers represent the highest accomplishment of the cabinetmaker's art. On other furniture, the Chippendale style's most basic characteristic is bold carving: seat backs are intricately shaped and pediments of case pieces and clocks are dramatic – with scrolls and finials standing out prominently. In addition, furniture of the period becomes more varied and comfortable and a new range of specialized pieces comes into existence. In short, it is the great age of the cabinetmaker.

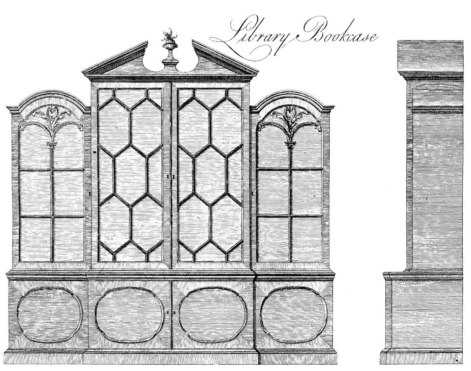

Library Bookcase

Above: A superb Charleston bookcase, probably used for the display of ceramics, with the Chippendale engraving that inspired it.

Among the contributions to southern comfort in the mid-18th Century was the so-called "French" chair, below right, later known as a "lolling" chair, and now more patriotically called a "Martha Washington" chair. *Left:* Designed for practicality rather than comfort, the convenience, or "close-stool" chair concealed a chamber pot beneath its slip seat.

Right: The most ubiquitous chair was the side chair (also known as a straight chair), and made with or without arms. Although mostly used for dining, they were also placed about parlors and other public rooms for the casual seating of guests. One might find as many as thirty or forty side chairs in a single large home and twice that number was not uncommon. In the Queen Anne years, the practice of using "slip" seats, that is, seat bottoms that could be removed to change the upholstery, came into fashion.

By the last half of the 18th Century, southern cabinetmakers had come a long way from the dark, ponderous court cupboards of early colonial days. A wide variety of so-called case furniture had come into use – ranging from daringly tall highboys, left, to impressively-carved lowboys, below, and sturdy, double-duty chests with desk tops whose drawer fronts were carved from single blocks of wood. Highboys are rare in the South and oddly enough, despite the large number of skilled cabinetmakers in Charleston, none at all are known to have been made there. However, stacked chests of drawers, usually in two sections, were common in Charleston: an uncommon variation is the mahogany triple chest at right. *Far right:* Equally rare is this magnificent walnut block-front desk, by an unknown North Carolina cabinetmaker.

39

Handsomely proportioned and exquisitely made, this Charleston chest-on-chest probably comes from the hand of Thomas Elfe. His distinguishing mark is the carved frieze of egg-and-diamond fretwork, below right. A form that seems unique to Charleston, this is a combination secretary-wardrobe. The top drawer of the lower section is false; when folded down on its elegant brass quadrant, the false front becomes a desk top, and the space behind it is fitted with pigeonholes and drawers. Made of mahogany with cypress as a secondary wood, the piece glistens with fine details, from its sturdy but graceful foot, below far right, (called a double ogee bracket) to its shining brasses. Interestingly, the metalwork may have been made in Charleston; although most domestic hardware was imported, it is known that a brass foundry was established in Charleston in 1760.

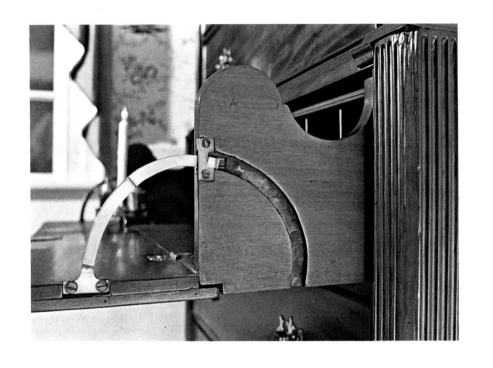

Although it seems that tea has been around forever, it was only in the early 18th Century that it became a fashionable drink. Furniture gradually evolved for use in the social ceremony of taking tea, and one of the most beautiful forms that emerged was the round, scallop-edged, tripod tea table. *Below, left:* This is a fine Charleston example; its top is shown tilted up as the table might have been stored against a wall. *Below, right:* A marble-top side table was a practical solution for the mixing of drinks.

Below: Thomas Elfe of Charleston also probably made the small, drop-leaf breakfast table, carving one end of the skirt with an open fretwork design that resembles his distinctive carving on the secretary-chest on the previous pages. The table's basic design, however, is borrowed from Chippendale's book. *Far left:* This table also displays a debt to Chippendale in the modified "Chinese" brackets at the tops of the legs.

While time may have seemed to move slowly in the Old South, it moved nevertheless, and every fashionable home had one or more clocks to intone the hours. Most were what are now called grandfather clocks; tall wooden cases housed the works. More rare were the compact shelf, or bracket, clocks. Clock cases were made by cabinetmakers, but, regrettably for furniture historians, the names on the dials of clocks are often those of the makers or purveyors of the mechanisms rather than the cabinetmakers. But one, at least, probably a folk craftsman in the Valley of Virginia, left his initials behind as part of a charming painted design.

The Federal era. By the time the Revolutionary War was concluded, another revolution had taken place in the decorative arts. This nonviolent rebellion had started in Europe, where a reaction against flamboyant, curvilinear earlier styles was leading to a greater simplicity of forms – a new classicism. And as the new American Republic asserted itself, the ordered regularity of straight lines, pediments and columns like those of ancient Rome, the use of shield backs for chairs, and the eagle as a design motif seemed wholly appropriate to the spirit of independence. In America, this is known as the Federal period. At left is an elegant dining room representative of the period; the woodwork is from a South Carolina house called White Hall. Interestingly, the mantel, cornice, and chair rail are carved in white pine, a wood not native to the South. The wood was imported by some cabinetmakers and builders because it is more easily carved than the local yellow pine. The chairs, with their Gothic arches, are from Charleston; the dining table, delicately inlaid with medallions and strings of bellflowers, was made in Baltimore. Similar detail enlivens the cellaret, shown drawn up to the table, with its mixing tray pulled out to hold a wine decanter.

Baltimore furniture of the Federal period is characterized by rich veneers, intricate inlays of light satinwood, and painted glass panels known as eglomise. The tall cylinder-front secretary in Winterthur's Baltimore drawing room is a supreme expression of the cabinetmaker's skill. Surmounted by a boldly carved eagle with an American shield on its breast, which is repeated on the inlay of the gracefully rounded desk top, the piece stands confidently on thin, tapering legs with tear-drop-shaped, satinwood inlays.

The American eagle also decorates the top of the candlestand below, which might have doubled as a firescreen in its tilted position. Of upholstered pieces of the period, few are more graceful than the easy chair at left or the cabriole-back sofa in the drawing room.

By the end of the 18th Century, the slant-top desk was being replaced by more sophisticated forms. The cylinder-fall desk, modeled after designs of Sheraton and Hepplewhite, was never highly popular but was the antecedent for the businessman's roll-top desk that became ubiquitous in the early 1900s. This handsome inlaid piece is a prime example of Baltimore craft. The lady's cabinet on page 5 is a related form: its popularity coincided with the rise in women's education.

Painted glass panels were a characteristic decorative form on Federal period furniture, mirrors and clocks. Inset on the surface like inlaid woods, the reverse side of the glass was painted in gold leaf or oil colors; the technique, often adopted as an amateur pastime, is called eglomise after the French designer, Jean Baptiste Glomi. This tall desk and bookcase from Baltimore shows both floral designs and a helmeted warrior based on a baroque painting by Salvator Rosa.

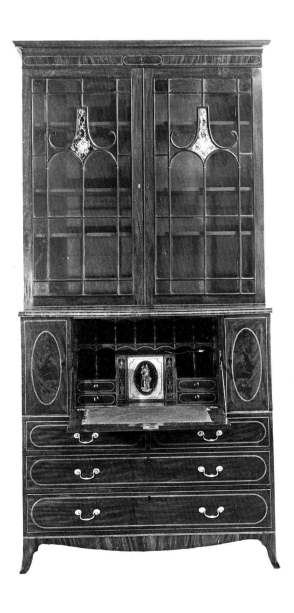

51

Satinwood geometric inlays decorate the cornice of this unusual Charleston high post bed; a local characteristic is the carving of rice stalks on the posts, identifying a crop on which the city grew rich. Also distinctive is the fact that the headboard lifts out, presumably to permit freer circulation of air in the sultry Carolina summers.

Rosewood and holly form the inlays on this mahogany bedstead from Virginia, whose square, tapering legs conform to the ideas of an influential English designer of the period, George Hepplewhite. His book *The Cabinetmaker's and Upholsterer's Guide* and a treatise by Thomas Sheraton contain the basis for the design of a great deal of furniture of the Federal period.

Maker's labels are rare on all American furniture, but in the South – so the speculation goes – even when a cabinetmaker pasted a paper label into his work, the humid climate and glue-eating insects destroyed it. More likely, the furniture was never marked. However, two labeled Charleston pieces by Robert Walker do exist. This clothes press by Walker features sliding trays on which folded clothing was stored, a characteristic also found in the armoires of Louisiana and Texas.

In addition to large storage furniture, southern cabinetmakers were called upon to make a variety of small, highly specialized pieces. The elegant little chest at left is inlaid with delicate stringing, and fitted with three tin canisters for tea and a lock surrounded by an ivory escutcheon. Tea was still a valuable commodity in the early 19th Century, hence the lock. *Right:* Medicinal herbs and other remedies were undoubtedly kept in this apothecary chest, probably a rural planter's first aid kit. Incidentally, both cabinets, though made late in the 18th Century, bear Chippendale-style bracket feet – an example of the kind of stylistic holdovers that characterize American furniture of all regions.

Billiards was a popular pastime in the early South. But oddly enough, the billiard table at the right is the only one remaining known to have been made in America before 1825. It is believed to be by John Shaw of Annapolis. Over eleven and a half feet long and six feet wide, the durable table is a tribute to Shaw's craft; unlike modern tables, the bed is not of slate but comprised of forty-five hard pine panels set in a complex, cross-braced framework.

Left: Because they were often gilded, looking glasses were frequently sold by picture framers and specialist importers of mirrored glass plate. This piece, called a dressing or "swing" glass, was kept atop a chest of drawers or dressing table; its glass tilts, and beneath it is a drawer for small personal effects. The simple but elegant form of the hand mirror was carved of mahogany.

This Charleston sewing stand is inlaid with maple, rosewood and cherry – an unusual complement of woods for a small piece. Also unusual for its kidney shape, the table is unique in having its cloth bag (for storing fabric remnants and clothing for repair) closely fitted to the legs.

Early in the days of the new nation, it was discovered that imported pianos frequently became unplayable, either because of the warping of wood due to the long sea voyage from Europe, or because of different climatic conditions here. Thus local makers – some of them immigrants already skilled in the work – were encouraged. In 1792, James Juhan advertised in a Richmond newspaper, enumerating in detail the problems and cost of importing pianos; then he declared his hope "that he may meet with some encouragement in manufacturing those delightful instruments . . . free from all the above defects. . . . The goodness of the work will show itself, as it will not be hidden, like those imported, under patched up fineers [sic] which soon fall in pieces." How well Juhan succeeded is not known, but the Baltimore makers represented here evidently had some success. At left is an interesting early version of the spinet or upright piano, with its stringboard exposed like a giant harp. *Far left:* The top view of the piano shows the conventional arrangement of the stringboard on instruments of this type. J. Stewart, maker of the piano at right, set his nameplate within an elaborate ormolu frame.

Painted furniture. From its earliest history, furniture was painted – for protection and decoration. Of course, when beautiful woods were employed, a transparent finish was applied to bring out the intricate grains and rich colors. But when economy called for simple woods, a painted finish was often added. Painting was done as an all-over, single color coating; in imitation of the grains of expensive woods or marble; and in the form of flowers, fruit, landscapes, and even historical or mythological tableaux. Often done as folk decoration – as on the blanket chest on page 17 or the clock on page 44 – painted furniture reached a high level of sophistication in the Federal period. Baltimore painted furniture, from about 1800 to 1840, is the finest to be found anywhere. And the leading decorators were the brothers John and Hugh Finlay, who created the pieces seen at left in the Oxford Parlor at the Museum of Early Southern Decorative Arts. Called "fancy furniture," painted pieces were bought by the richest merchants though they could afford mahogany or other costly woods. Most Baltimore fancy furniture consists of chairs, settees and small tables; very few large case pieces were made, probably because painted decoration over large surfaces seemed awkward. But the chairs, settees and tables are marvels of lightness and delicacy.

Bolton Mount Deposit

Grace Hill Montebello

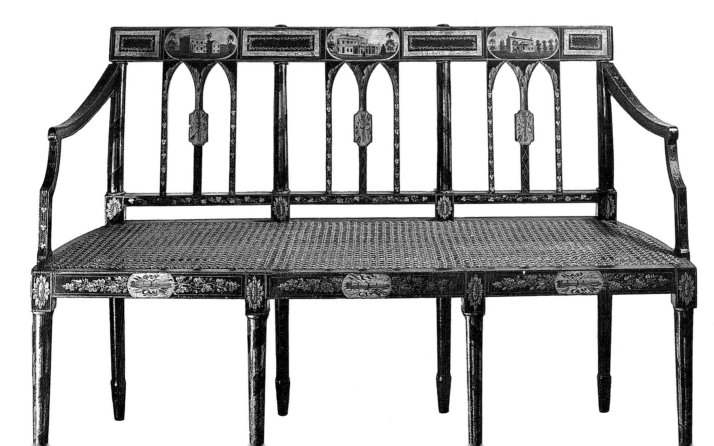

62

Homewood
Banks of the City of Baltimore

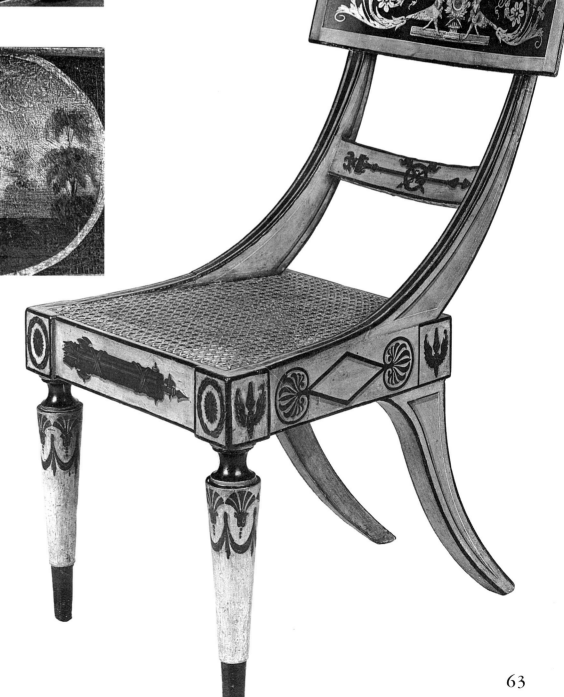

Luxurious homes and major buildings of the city were a popular motif for the designs painted on Baltimore fancy furniture. Why anyone would want a chair ornamented with someone else's house, or a hospital or bank, remains puzzling – but there is no doubt that it was the taste of the time. The settee at the left is from a famous thirteen-piece suite, containing two settees, ten chairs and a marble-topped pier table. The chairs and table each picture one notable Baltimore building; the settees display three architectural portraits. Oddly, none of the buildings seem to have had any special connection with the man who ordered the set, John Morris, a merchant. Of the seventeen buildings portrayed, two remain standing in Baltimore: Homewood is on the grounds of Johns Hopkins University; Mount Clare is in a city park.

Styles of the Piedmont. The best early writer on the cultural history of the South, Carl Bridenbaugh, identified three major social regions. On the populous coast were the Chesapeake and Carolina societies. Both, by virtue of easy access to the sea, were closely tied to England and to the northern colonies. Their furniture, therefore, tended to follow standard lines. Because the area was rich, the work was usually luxurious. Inland was the Piedmont or Back Country region, loosely comprising everything from western Virginia down through the Carolinas into Georgia and westward as far as Tennessee and Kentucky. The most obvious feature of Piedmont furniture is its lack of sophistication, though the makers were far from unskilled. They were aware of the changes of fashion experienced on the coast, but tended to adopt them later and to hold on longer to older forms. (The Windsor chair seen in this dining room was popular from about 1725 to the middle of the 19th Century.) They were also somewhat freer in interpreting designs. But these adaptations are what gives Piedmont furniture its charm. Back Country makers also used native materials exclusively: in the room at left, the drop-leaf table is walnut, and its inlays are maple. The painted woodwork in the room, inspired by Robert Adam in England, is freely adapted; the oval floral design on the marbleized chimney and the framed relief below the mantle *(details below)* are original touches.

Left: John Swisegood, one of the finest (and one of the few identified) Piedmont cabinetmakers, signed this masterful desk when he was nearing the end of his apprenticeship and not yet twenty-one years old. Distinctive Swisegood touches on the basically Hepplewhite form are "comma" inlays at the corners of the drawers, the use of burl walnut banding and striped inlays and the delicate splayed feet. In the chest below, the use of cherry wood and the light and dark barber-pole inlays are distinctive Kentucky characteristics. Made in 1810, the piece echoes an earlier style in its modified Queen Anne cabriole legs – a true Piedmont attribute.

Travellers' Rest, in Nashville, Tennessee, was formerly the home of Judge John Overton, a colleague of Andrew Jackson. Today it houses a fine collection of southern furniture dating from about 1810. In the Judge's bedroom, at right, the chest by the window is made entirely of walnut; the walnut desk has poplar as a secondary wood. The pencil posts of the rope-strung canopy bed are of ash.

66

Not surprisingly, the two distinctive furniture forms of the South – the cellaret on legs and the huntboard – are both associated with the Southerner's traditional reputation for good living, hospitality, and a love for fine food and plentiful drink. Exactly how the sideboard differs from the similar huntboard often found in dining rooms (like that at left) depends largely on the viewer's experience. No definite rules apply. Most agree, however, that the huntboard should be taller (above forty inches), shallower, contain fewer drawers, and be less sophisticated in style and manufacture. Indeed, the prototypical huntboard was probably nothing more than a long board on high legs, for its use dictated its form; as far as one knows, it was intended to serve a group of thirsty, hungry men as they stood on the back porch or in the center hall of a plantation house on their way to or from a long day's chase. Dressed for hunting and perhaps muddy as well, they would be less welcome sitting at the dining table than standing beside the huntboard, refreshing themselves with food and a julep. In any case, the huntboard/sideboards on these pages (others are seen in the Tennessee dining room on page 16 and in the billiard room on page 57) run the gamut of styles and types.

Like tea, coffee and spices, sugar was an extremely valuable commodity in the Old South. Usually sold in tall, solid cones – from which a day's needs were chipped or scraped – and wrapped in scarlet or blue paper, sugar was often kept in locked "safes," which were sometimes displayed in the sitting room. In the room at left from Travellers' Rest, a cherry and poplar sugar chest stands near the fireplace. The two chests, made in the early 19th Century, are also of cherry; the one on the right has sides of curly maple. *Below:* A small chest from Tennessee bears a delightful inlay of a brick house – a design resembling samplers of the time. Its size probably indicates that it was intended to stand on a sideboard.

These beds from the Piedmont are essentially simple frames strung with ropes to support a crude mattress. *Left:* The trundle bed is a space-saving form that was stored under a high double bed during the day and then rolled out at night; older children usually slept in them. The cradle below, constructed of walnut, comes from Virginia or North Carolina; some cradles, like the one on page 75, have pegs along their side rails so that an infant can be laced in for safety. The curious object at the right, just over fifteen inches long, was used to tighten the ropes of a bed when they began to sag. The notch was slipped over the rope, a rod was slipped through the hole at the top, and the whole "bed wrench" was twisted to bring up the tension. Both beds at the right have rope frames; the one below is a superb 1750s Queen Anne-style Moravian bed; above is a handsome Kentucky bedstead of cherry.

By 1820, the Moravian community of Salem in the Piedmont of North Carolina was a thriving center where craftsmen of all kinds flourished. One of its leading artisans was John Vogler, a silversmith, clockmaker, and master of numerous other mechanical arts. His shop was in the front room on the ground floor of his home. This comfortable bedroom from Vogler's house contains some furniture believed to have been made by him. It demonstrates that he was a dab hand at woodwork, in addition to his other accomplishments. Here, the rocker and armchair, resembling Windsor chairs, contain bent hickory armrests and other elements that are ingeniously formed, probably steamed into a pliable state and shaped on a mold. No other such examples are known. Much of the other furniture in the room is of local manufacture, though not by Vogler himself. Especially notable are the tester bed, the cradle and the commodious poplar linen press.

One of the most remarkable styles of furniture and object design indigenous to America was that of the Shakers, a communal religious sect founded in this country in 1774 by a dissident English Quaker, Mother Ann Lee. The first Shaker community in the South was in Pleasant Hill, Kentucky; it was established in 1806. The following year a community called South Union was founded in Kentucky's Logan County, and both thrived as farming and craft communities until late in the century. Shaker craftsmanship embodies three prime qualities – harmony, simplicity and practicality. It was said by Shakers that a chair should be "fit for an angel to sit upon." Shaker cabinetmakers did not rely on carved or painted adornment to enhance their furniture; the simple harmony of well-proportioned parts, with the occasional addition of a modest pattern in a woven chair seat, for example, suffices to create their beauty. The practicality is evident everywhere. In these rooms, peg rails along the walls serve to hang candle sconces, clothing and chairs (so that floors may be swept more easily); built-in cupboards and drawers save space, and a double desk was designed to seat two workers at once. The Shakers disprove the notion that clean, spare design is a product of the 20th Century.

In the Deep South. When King Cotton began dispensing his beneficence, planters and merchants furnished their spacious mansions with imported goods. They not only gathered furniture abroad but they acquired pieces in Philadelphia and New York. One Natchez mansion was built of brick imported from England. For another, the owner hired a Philadelphia architect, ordered the house built in "oriental" style, and sent to Philadelphia for every stick of furniture. Typical of the preferred decor of the period is the parlor at left, from the beautiful Natchez house D'Evereux, built in 1840, and furnished with a rosewood suite ordered from Cincinnati. As a result of this penchant for "imports," a tradition of fine cabinetmaking failed to develop in much of the Deep South. Only New Orleans, with its rich French tradition, gave birth to an indigenous style and produced two great craftsmen, Prudent Mallard and Francois Seignoret, and their schools of followers. Elsewhere, local artisans fashioned useful and attractive, if not trend-setting, furniture which satisfied their clients and honored their profession. The armoire below, for example, made by an anonymous cabinetmaker for a Woodville, Mississippi client combines a French form with Hepplewhite feet and inlays more characteristic of the Carolinas or Kentucky.

In 1822 there were more than fifty cabinetmakers, four carvers and gilders, five chair makers, and twenty-two upholsterers listed in the New Orleans city directory. Their names are known, yet what they made remains frustratingly undocumented. This handsome chest of drawers, for example, with its acanthus carving, marble top, and oval serpentine mirror can only be identified as a product of the "school of Mallard," not definitely as a work of the great Prudent Mallard. Mallard and Francois Seignoret are the two finest New Orleans makers, yet their specific works are almost entirely unknown.

The fine New Orleans house known as "Madame John's Legacy" has been restored to show various Louisiana life-styles from 1788 to the 1830s. *Left:* The library contains early country-style furniture. The armoire was made from walnut and cypress. Containing its original leather seat, the sling chair speaks of the region; simple rush-bottomed chairs and a rough table round out the furnishings. *Right:* In this living room are a high-style sofa and side chairs attributed to Seignoret. A Sheraton-style gaming table stands beneath a large piece of French toile once used for drapery material in the house.

Plantation furniture is a romantic but inaccurate term for much back country furniture throughout the South. It is most unlikely, for example, that a plantation carpenter could have built the substantial "planter's desk" at left or the elegantly proportioned, French-style table (with its doe feet) below. On the other hand, the bed at the far left, made of cypress with detachable poles to hold mosquito netting, could well have been knocked together by a handy carpenter, as could the cradle. *Far right:* This chair, with its seat of woven twisted cornshucks, was made in Alachua County, Florida, in 1850. *Above, right:* This country-made Louisiana chair is modeled on the Louis XVI style of the late 18th Century; it is an ingenious local adaptation of a very fancy design.

The chairs below and in the bedroom at left reveal the beautiful form of the designs of Francois Seignoret. Tucked behind these mahogany pillars of Gothic Revival style, and gazing up at the pleated fabric "sky," one could not fail to have pleasant dreams. The high (nine feet, eight inches) canopy attests to the capacious ceilings of Louisiana homes of the 1840s and is typical of New Orleans beds sold throughout the Mississippi Valley.

Right: Marking its link with New Orleans, a pleated satin "sky" decorates the front of this unique, disguised desk made of rosewood and pine about 1840. Said to double as a firescreen, the piece seems too large for that purpose; but when the satin-covered front is lowered, its real function as a writing desk is revealed.

Trade between back country Tennessee and Kentucky and the lower Mississippi Valley was brisk even before steamboats began to ply the river in 1811. By 1820 some sixty boats were shuttling goods between New Orleans and Ohio. Overland, the Natchez Trace linked the areas. Therefore, to find Louisiana furniture in a Tennessee house should not be surprising. But coupled with this is the fact that the house belonged to Judge John Overton, a law partner of Andrew Jackson – hero of the Battle of New Orleans. This is the upstairs bedroom of Overton's Nashville home, Travellers' Rest. Prominently seen under the window is a Seignoret chair; the distinctive Louisiana sling seat variously called a Spanish, bootjack, bautac, or Campeachy chair and a New Orleans armoire are beside it. Evidence for its original presence in the house – which was stripped of all its furnishings by Union troops in 1864 – lies in an inventory made by Overton that lists a "Spanish chair," perhaps a duplicate of this one, covered in red leather.

East Texas furniture. The presence of German craftsmen accounts for most of the furniture built in Texas from the late 1830s to the turn of the century. And the workmanship has a special character. Generally solid and simple, the furniture conforms little to the fashions of England and France that dominated most other American styles. It combines a kind of Germanic precision and practicality with a western American feeling for size and strength; the furniture utilizes decorative details that speak both of origins and of adopted symbols. In the chest of drawers at left, for example, the carving around each keyhole (called an escutcheon) combines a traditional leaf pattern with a scroll resembling those at the corners of the piece. But the scroll above the escutcheon looks more like a pair of horns! Less subtle by far is the furniture actually made from horns that became popular in the 1880s. Flamboyant, self-confident, and proud in its use of local materials, this furniture could only have come from Texas and, like it or not, it has the courage of its convictions. At its best, it rings another note in the varied harmony of regional America.

With the exception of horn furniture, most Texas pieces follow standard forms such as the desk on chest of drawers below or the highpost bed. The rawhide seat of the rocking chair at left attests to its true Texas origin. Daybeds seem especially popular, perhaps because of the hot climate and as a holdover from the Mexican/Spanish tradition of the siesta. *Left:* This daybed is especially notable because it expands into a double bed; the mattress unfolds to cover the extended frame. Mostly, Texas cabinetmakers – some of whom doubled as wheelwrights and wagon builders – made conventional pieces, one of the most popular being the armoire. *Right:* This decorative armoire, however, has a look of its own, reminiscent of a Gothic cathedral; its closest parallels are the Jacobean pieces shown on pages 18-19, with their applied, half-round decoration and molded doors. The piece dates from 1880 however; perhaps it was inspired by the revival of interest in early American life that was sparked by the nation's Centennial celebrations in 1876.

A furniture form less common to other parts of the South but especially familiar in Louisiana and Texas is the food safe. It is a large, shelved cabinet with open panels set with either pierced tin sheets or screens made of wire or cheesecloth. (The screens on the food safe below have been removed.) Presumably, the greater number of insect pests in the area occasioned the need for this storage piece.

The rooms above and at the right are in the McGregor-Grimm house near Austin, named for its two most prominent owners. *Above:* An upstairs sitting room was probably used as a workroom as the desk and the sewing machine at the window suggest. *Right:* The painted, false-grained walls and doors in the downstairs entrance hall give the house its special character. Evidently done by an immigrant German artist called Melchior, the painting provides the space with oak and rosewood wainscoting, classical columns, and paneled doors – all delightfully fraudulent.

Right: Furnished with a suite of pieces – sofa, rocker, and center table – by the German-American craftsman, Friderich Christofer Carl Steinhagen, the parlor of the McGregor-Grimm house is one of the most pleasant rooms in the South. *Below:* Melchior's ceiling painting, done partly in stencil and partly freehand, plays fast and loose with realism but lends an air of lightness and gaiety to the room. The furniture, too, with its swan's head armrests on the sofa and rocker and a pair of unlikely reclining fish atop the back rail of the sofa, adds a touch of whimsy and fun to this unpretentious and lively living space. And perhaps the best mark of what is truly American in this country's decorative arts is the room's history: ordered by a second generation North Carolinian of Scottish descent, decorated by a German only recently arrived in the New World, and now furnished with pieces made by a man who earned his living as a wheelwright, it seems a true melting pot of influences.

Left: Dominating this downstairs bedroom is a black walnut bed made by Johann Umland in 1861 for a Washington County planter.

Art of the silversmith. Though silver was probably relatively more expensive in earlier times than it is today, there exists an astonishing amount of it. Although the Civil War saw much southern silver leave the South in the saddlebags of Union officers, plenty remains, a surprising amount in fact. From early colonial times, many silversmiths worked below the Mason-Dixon line. Though southern silver shows few of the regional characteristics that mark the more abundant northern work, a complete range of forms was made – everything from simple tankards and cups to baroque pieces like the wine wagon below, made in Charleston. Common objects, of course, were the various pieces of a tea service – sugar and creamers, tongs, waste bowls, spoons, and round-bodied teapots as well as tall coffee pots. Most common were the cups sometimes called beakers, and now known as julep cups. Southern silver is similar in style to that made elsewhere – from the early, simple forms of the 18th Century, through the classical Federal period, to a more highly ornate silver which became popular at the end of the 19th Century. Usually marked only with the maker's name, southern silver like most American silver does not have the complete information revealing the quality, date, and place that the hallmarks of English silver give to the connoisseur. Only Baltimore adopted an assay system.

A pair of silver goblets by William Ball of Baltimore.

Although not the oldest known objects of silver made in the South, these represent the earliest style known in southern workmanship: a boldly curvaceous baroque mode that parallels the lines of Queen Anne furniture. The sinuous scroll handle of the mug at left is characteristic. The most common early decorative motif, the shell, unites this group, seen in the silver and mother-of-pearl snuffbox, the legs of the sauceboat, the spout of the coffee pot, and the bowl of the ladle. Shoe buckles were one of the first items of personal use made in silver in this country; the one at left dates from about 1780.

By the end of the 18th Century, the ornate Baroque style was giving way to the simpler, more classical feeling of what has come to be known as the Federal style. An elegant example of this is the columnar form of the single candlestick at right. *Left:* The brilliant, clear expanse of smooth silver of this soup tureen made by Charles Louis Boehme of Baltimore in about 1800 marks one of the masterpieces of the silversmith's art in the Federal period. The refined lines of Federal silver are also evident in pieces from the recently settled state of Kentucky, represented here by the ladle and spoon at the left and the beaker and pair of candlesticks at the right. The teaspoon and candlesticks were made by Kentucky's most famous silversmith, Asa Blanchard, and were owned by Isaac Shelby, the first Governor of Kentucky and a hero of the Battle of King's Mountain. The form of the beaker would later become famous as the most suitable container for Kentucky's popular drink, the mint julep.

Tea serving pieces were the most common forms of fancy silver in the average household. By the 19th Century, the drinking of tea and the polite social ceremony that accompanied it had become nearly as ingrained in the American mind as in some Oriental societies. As many as nineteen pieces could comprise a tea service – everything from sugar tongs, waste bowls and strainers to the more familiar pots and creamers, as well as a matched set of a dozen or more teaspoons. *Left:* These pieces are by Standish Barry, a noted Baltimore maker who, like many of his colleagues, also did business as a watch and clockmaker. Versatility was also the strong suit of the Moravian craftsman John Vogler, who made the teaspoons at the right (a wedding ring he made for his wife appears on page 108). Virginia's Matthew Cluff was responsible for the elegant sugar and creamer above . These beautifully matched pieces show the marvelous quality of silver, the subtle shapes into which it can be hammered, and the lustrous sheen that the rounded and sharp-edged forms reflect.

103

104

Some of the most beautiful silver was made as gifts for war heroes or distinguished public servants. *Far left:* This model of a fireman's megaphone was given to the chief of a volunteer fire company in Louisville in 1843. The beaker beside it, by Kentucky's Asa Blanchard, was offered as a prize at an agricultural fair. Also from Kentucky is the heavily decorated pitcher, made by William Kendrick of Louisville, and presented to Major W. E. Woodruff by his rifle battalion in 1860. *Far right:* The knife and scabbard were also made for a military man, a Major Brahan, by the noted San Antonio silversmith Samuel Bell. *Above:* Naval hero Stephen Decatur received the elegantly sculptured silver salver from the grateful citizens of Baltimore, who had commissioned Andrew Ellicott Warner to make it in 1817. Surely, however, no one received more costly gifts and tributes than the French hero of the American Revolution, Lafayette. When Lafayette returned to America in 1824 and made a triumphal tour of the States, he was showered with gifts from an admiring public. *Right:* The Governor of South Carolina, in the name of the citizenry, presented Lafayette with this map case on his visit to Columbia in March, 1825. Made by L. Boudo, the case is fittingly engraved "In tracing your route through our Territory every inhabited spot will recall to your memory the devotion and affection of a grateful people."

A more elaborate style of decoration on silver became popular in the 1830s and continued in vogue throughout most of the 19th Century. On holloware serving pieces, the principal means of such decorations was the repoussé technique: the silver sheet was raised by hammering it from behind, creating a rich relief on the surface. *Right:* This goblet, sold by the firm of Hyde and Goodrich of New Orleans, demonstrates the method. At this time the repertoire of the silversmith was also expanded with the introduction of new serving pieces. The cake server at the far left — made by a transplanted New Yorker, James Conning of Mobile — and the luncheon or dessert fork at left from the Macon, Georgia shop of William Blackstone Johnston reveal a new, sophisticated array of equipment for entertaining. Knives like the one at the left, by Andrew Warner of Baltimore, with its baroque hollow handle, are unusual from as early as 1828; they frequently wore out because of hard use. Of all the high style decorators of silver, however, none was better known, or more dramatic in his use of repoussé technique, than Samuel Kirk of Baltimore, founder of a firm that continues to this day as the oldest surviving silversmiths in the United States. The kettle, stand and lamp are part of an exquisite seven-piece set made by S. Kirk and Son in the 1850s.

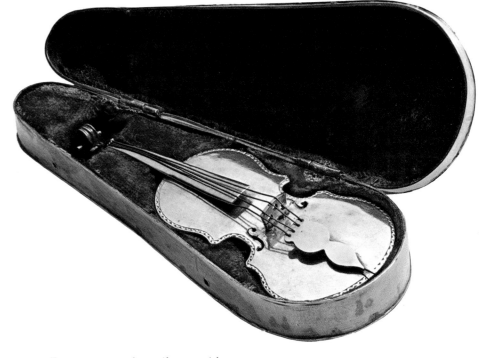

Far more rare than silver, gold was nonetheless widely used by southern jewelers and silversmiths. *Upper left:* The gold medal was presented to General Lafayette on his triumphal visit to Baltimore on October 11, 1824. Another Frenchman, Jacob Esterle, was a silversmith in Kentucky from 1835 to 1868; he made the charming gold and silver violin – the case is just over three inches long – in about 1862. Its purpose remains unknown. A clear sentiment is attached, however, to the delightful wedding ring made by the talented John Vogler for his bride Christina Spach in 1819. Formed of three bands, the ring shows a pair of clasped hands when closed; when opened, a double heart is revealed, which bears the inscription "With God and Thee My Joy Shall Be." The Texas silversmith Samuel Bell – who made the knife on page 105 – decorated this pocket watch for a cattleman. The works were made in the North, but Bell created the real value of the piece in chased borders representing grasses and in the figure of a longhorn.

A wealth of ceramics. Plates, pitchers, cups, bottles and bowls are such integral parts of a family's daily life that it is inconceivable to do without them. And so, from the earliest colonial times, potters were among the first craftsmen to set up shop in the South. But they could not begin to supply the needs of the many rapidly growing communities. Therefore, from the start, and well into the 19th Century, ceramic ware was imported. Not only England but France, Germany, and especially China contributed shiploads of ceramics to the southern market. Some of it was made especially for sale here and showed local scenes and historical figures. Much was simply the standard run, which makers knew they could dispose of in America because their prices were better. The price advantage became less and less a factor, however, as American potters began tooling up for larger production. Fortunately the South was not short of materials; fine clays exist widely, and Josiah Wedgwood and other English potters actually experimented with some American clays. The only thing southern makers were never able to produce with success was porcelain.

Moravian master potter Gottfried Aust even made his shop sign of earthenware.

An unusual and charming piece of European porcelain made expressly for the southern market, this vase is one of a pair showing a view of Baton Rouge from across the Mississippi. They were commissioned by a wealthy cotton broker, who ordered them from the Fischer Porcelain Works in Pirkenhammer, Bohemia in about 1860. The source for the scenic view used by the porcelain painters was an engraved map of lower Mississippi plantations (a detail of which is shown right) done by the New Orleans artist Marie Adrien Persac.

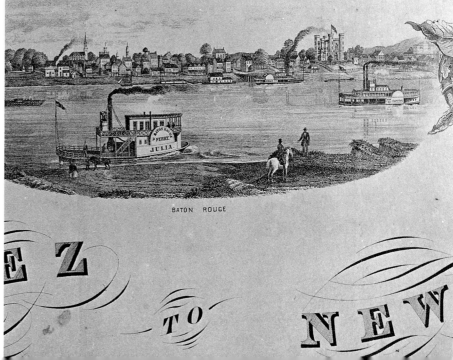

BATON ROUGE

Z TO NEW

These pieces of English porcelain were made for the southern trade — one on speculation and the other on commission. *Above:* The gravy boat was produced by John and William Ridgway sometime before 1830 as part of a series of ceramic works called "Beauties of America;" the view is of the Bank of Savannah. *Left:* This rare bowl was made by the Bow porcelain works in about 1768 and was part of an order of ceramic serving pieces commissioned by the Masonic Lodge of Hallifax, North Carolina.

113

Earthenware's varied forms. Numerous potters flourished throughout the South, but nowhere for so long or with such success as in the Moravian villages of Bethabara and Salem, in the Piedmont section of North Carolina known as Wachovia. Arriving in 1753 from Germany and Bohemia via Pennsylvania, the Moravians brought to colonial settlement not only a unique communal way of life and a devout and pacificist philosophy, but a high degree of skill in a variety of crafts. Pottery was one of the first needs of the new settlement. Good fine-grained local clay was readily available; flint and kaolin for making glazes could also be found nearby, and only the glaze additive red-lead had to be bought. Most of what the Moravians made was simple earthenware, the relatively brittle, low-fired clay product they adorned with simple glazes and free-flowing slip decoration in colors. Later, some of the Salem potters experimented with the bright, white pottery that the English called "Queens Ware," but very little of it remains. Because of the much higher kiln temperatures needed, the more highly refined clays, and the competition of cheap goods from abroad, no porcelain was attempted. *Left and below:* This gallery of Moravian pottery was mostly made by the first Salem master Gottfried Aust and Rudolf Christ, his successor.

Moravian settlers continued the European practice of heating their homes with tile stoves rather than open fireplaces. More efficient in their consumption of fuel, tile stoves also required less masonry and were easier to install than full fireplaces. As a result, stove tiles were among the first products of the Moravian potters. At far right is a stove with glazing that gives the effect of marble, a popular early pattern. Below is the last type of stove made by Moravians – classical moldings and acanthus leaves mark it as mid-19th Century in style.

An abundant supply of good, native clay and a rich tradition of pottery making brought by another group of immigrant German craftsmen made the Shenandoah Valley an outstanding center for earthenware throughout the 19th Century. The Bell family, beginning with patriarch Peter Bell about 1805, spanned the next 100 years. The Bells' production was large and varied, and their work attracted a wide and appreciative audience. *Below:* The plate, nearly two feet across and with substantial handles on the underside, was made by Peter Bell himself. *Left:* Son Solomon, who moved from Winchester, Virginia, to Strasburg to join his brother Samuel in business, produced the salt-glaze decorated water cooler. In 1882 the company name became S. Bell & Son; this identifying mark is on the shapely green and white vase at right.

Pottery making in Baltimore had a long history that culminated in the huge output of the Edwin Bennett works in the late 19th Century. Earlier, numerous smaller potteries thrived. *Above:* Here are two examples of stoneware – earthenware fired to a high temperature so the clay fuses and becomes hard and long-lasting. The pitcher bears the potter's name ("Morgan maker") around the throat; the base is marked with the pottery address and date. The other object, unfamiliar in these days of ballpoint pens, is a sand caster, used to sprinkle sand or pumice on fresh ink to dry it after writing.

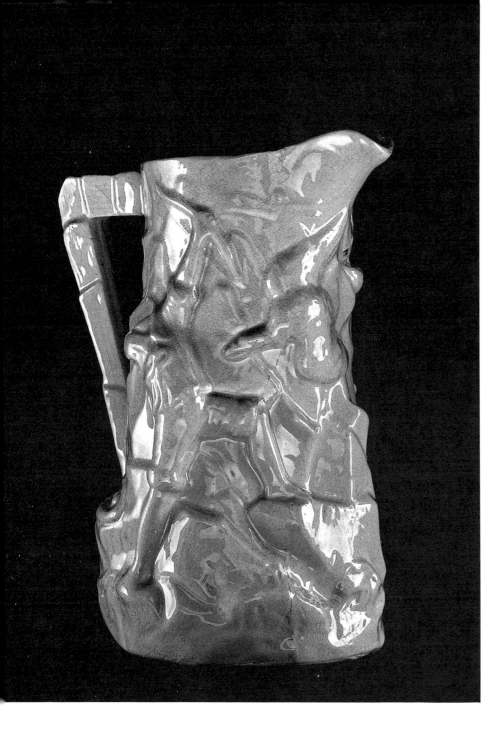

Edwin Bennett, in his long career in Baltimore, experimented with many kinds of pottery. *Left, above:* Here is one of his earlier pieces, a white stoneware pitcher with a molded scene of a hunter taking eggs from an eagle's nest. Bennett never succeeded in producing porcelain. Whether it was ever produced in the South is debatable; the pitcher above was made by the Southern Porcelain Company in South Carolina, but it is almost certainly not porcelain; it resembles Bennett's white stoneware. *Left:* Elsewhere in South Carolina, in Edgefield County, simpler earthenware was made by a number of potters, in attractive, original designs.

121

Two unusual art potteries were founded just before the turn of this century in the New Orleans area. In character and product they could not have been more different. The older, an outgrowth of the New Orleans Art Pottery Company, eventually became an adjunct of the fine women's school, Sophie Newcomb College of Tulane University. One of the men hired to make the ceramics that the women decorated eventually became a distinctive, if not distinguished, art potter himself. He was George Ohr, whose Biloxi Art Pottery was a fixture of the town for many years. Ohr actually gave up pottery in 1906, having created well over six thousand unique pieces (his earlier production had been destroyed in a fire in 1893). Though Ohr lived off the sale of commercial ware — chimney pots, planters, cooking utensils — his art pottery was his obsession. He thought he was the greatest potter in the world, and advertised himself as such. History's judgment is likely to be more reserved, but for sheer invention, technical genius (Ohr was able to make astonishingly thin-walled pieces) and for an exuberant personality, he is likely to be remembered. Among his work shown here is a double-spouted tea and coffee pot. The Newcomb work is more conservative in form but much more sophisticated in design. Essentially, the girls took animal and flower forms for motifs: as one student put it, "The whole thing was to be a southern product, made of southern clays, by southern artists, decorated with southern subjects."

Glass. With more optimism than foresight, the Jamestown colonists tried to build a glasshouse in the new land. By 1608, a group of Dutch and Polish workers were turning out glass, but in types that still remain unknown. The pioneering venture failed. But in 1621 – this time with Italian workmen – the colonists tried again. Their failure proved the end of American glassmaking for over a century and a half. Another southern glass factory was established when local authorities in Frederick, Maryland, persuaded John Frederick Amelung to leave his native Bremen in the 1780s. Amelung arrived with sixty-eight workers and equipment for three furnaces. Within six months, he was turning out window glass and bottles – staples of all early glassworks – but it took him six years to learn to deal with American materials and conditions and to produce fine, clear glass suitable for engraving. By the time he did, the high expenditures of setting up his plant and competition from abroad forced him to shut down. But in their ten years of work, the New Bremen artisans produced some wonderful objects: among them is the amethyst-colored covered sugar bowl on the title page. Amelung's influence did not die with his plant, however, for his workers moved on and enriched the glass industry in Baltimore, West Virginia, Kentucky, and Pennsylvania.

Left: Hobbs, Brockunier & Company made this "coin" glass. *Above:* Locally made "pig" bottles advertised a Louisville saloon.

Amelung sent this goblet to Germany to show that his enterprise was flourishing. The engraving reads "Old Bremen Success and the New Progress."

Known as a "pokal," this handsome covered wine goblet was made for Frederick William Marshall, administrator of the Moravian settlement in North Carolina.

This "case" bottle is one of a dozen Amelung made for Colonel Baker Johnson of Maryland in 1788. The square shape fitted the rectangular compartments of cellarets.

Amelung gave this flask to Francis Stanger, a New Jersey glassmaker. Symbols relate to Stanger: a bottle for his profession, a plow for New Jersey, and Masonic emblems.

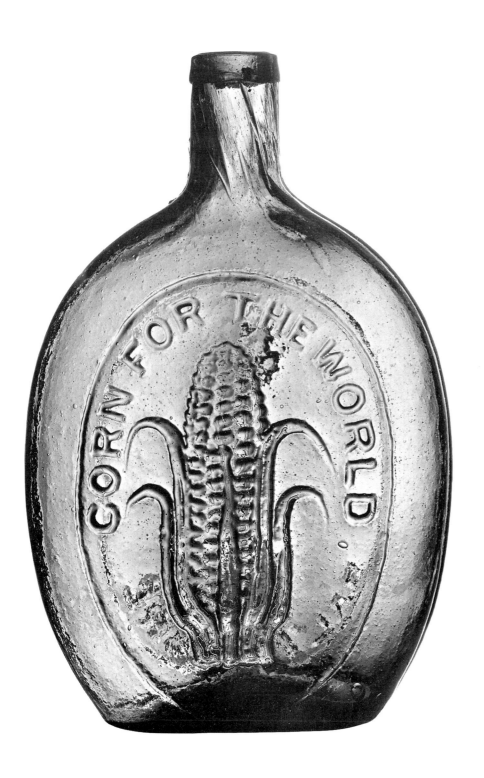

In addition to plain, utilitarian containers, the workers in Baltimore and Kentucky turned out decorative bottles made by blowing molten glass into design molds. Among the many popular images – including portraits of Washington and Zachary Taylor – were the "Corn for the World" slogan produced in Baltimore and the violin or scroll pattern, popular in Louisville. (The corn slogan celebrated the repeal of the British Corn laws of 1848, which levied high tariffs on imported grain.) Made in many sizes, these flasks were used for storing a variety of liquids besides whiskey. Before 1870, whiskey was not sold in individual bottles but put up in barrels or crocks.

Two other techniques of glassmaking were used to produce the handsome candlestick and windowpane shown here. The candlestick was formed by blowing glass into a pattern mold, removing it, and continuing the blowing to expand the pattern. The windowpane was made with a technique new in the 1820s, whereby hot glass was pressed mechanically into a mold. In this case, the mold was incised with a floral design and the background was stippled with small dots to reflect light. This type of glass, generally known as "pressed lacy," became very popular. The steamboat design from West Virginia, probably representing an Ohio River packet boat, is rare.

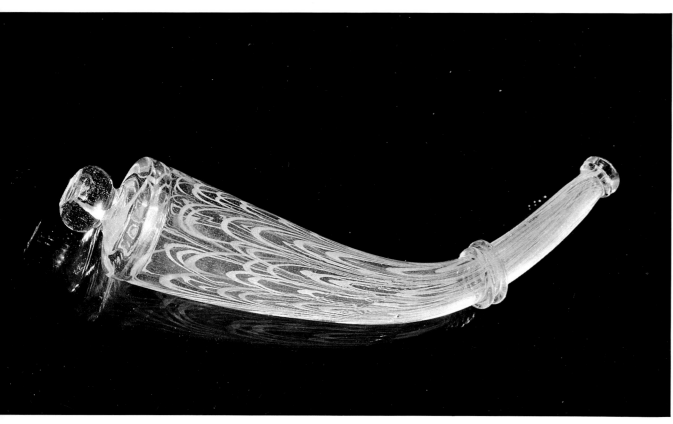

By the end of the 19th Century, industrial methods had been applied to glassmaking. A tradition and an appetite for fine art glass was continued, however, by a few makers. The leading southern art glass house — with a national reputation — was Hobbs, Brockunier and Company of Wheeling, West Virginia. They turned out a wide range of the colorful, flamboyant pieces, right, so prized in Victorian households. One of their most successful and artistic products came to be known as Wheeling Peachblow above. Peachblow was made with an outer body ranging in color from yellow to burgundy and an inner shell of opaque white to enhance the shading. It was actually intended as an imitation of Chinese porcelain. The vase at center with a separate, molded base of dragons' heads was a copy of the famous Morgan vase, a Chinese piece that had been sold at auction for the then astounding sum of $18,000. A glassblower's creative impulse is charmingly shown in the cornucopia at left; it is a so-called "whimsy," blown at the end of a day from remnant glass by an anonymous worker at a Kentucky glass factory. Many such pieces were produced, and usually given as gifts by the glassblowers themselves.

Objects of utility and commerce

The outside kitchen of the Brush-Everard House at Colonial Williamsburg.

No less interesting than the fine furniture, silver, ceramics and glass of the Old South are the objects of daily life – tools, textiles, hunting gear and trade goods. These things were crafted by skilled hands – those of farm women, town tradesmen and itinerant workers. Though the objects have never been valued for any intrinsic worth and have had little status in the marketplace of antiques, they are increasingly sought for what they reveal of living patterns of the past and as artifacts of craftsmanship. Seldom signed by their makers, these objects nevertheless bear the stamp of their origin in subtle ways; the manner of braiding a hickory splint basket, or the clever cuts and crimps of the tinsmith's shears on a candleholder. Nor have these skills been lost: for in various restorations of the South – from Williamsburg and Salem to Westville, Georgia – one can see the living tradition. And the importance of doing so is not only to know the articles better for seeing them put together or used, but to study the nature of craftsmen's tools and their techniques. It is also possible, then, to sense in a real way the time and care it took to make things. This is the ultimate lesson of many of the objects: what they tell of the pace of life in the past, of attention to detail, of the physical demands of having to make nearly everything one needed. In the textile section here, for example, one may be stimulated to think of the long and laborious process of making even such simple homespun bed covers as those shown in the Piedmont bedroom on page 154: first, cut the flax when it has grown sufficiently tall, crush it to break up the fibers, card it to separate them, spin handful after handful into hundreds of yards of yarn; pick the plants and fruits for dye pigments; grind, boil and distill them for purity; cut wood to heat the dye pot, boil the water, mix the dyes, soak the yarn and dry it; string the loom and weave the cloth. Even such a shorthand description of the process should be enough to endow the ancient craft with the greatest dignity.

Of nearly equal interest for the student of southern antiques is the world of commerce and business. Here, the artifacts are not often handmade but they nevertheless speak eloquently of time gone by and a different way of life. In all honesty, it cannot be said that southern commercial artifacts are much different from those found elsewhere, but there are distinctive southern products whose history is worth preserving. Not the least important of these are three of the nation's most popular soft drinks – Dr. Pepper, Coca-Cola and Pepsi Cola. Whiskey, too, has been a familiar and desired product of the South – bourbon being the specialty. One could hardly ignore tobacco, the plant on which much of the South's earliest wealth was founded. The growing and marketing of tobacco – and cotton to a lesser extent – generated a large number of artifacts, especially huge quantities of printed advertising, containers, labels. Finally, in this survey of useful objects, must come the weapons and adjuncts of hunting, and their other application as implements of war. Most famous, of course, is the Kentucky rifle, which interestingly was hardly ever made in that state: named for the "long hunters" who traveled as far as Kentucky for furs, the rifles were mostly made in Maryland, North Carolina, Virginia and (to be honest) Pennsylvania. As articles of utility, fashioned with care and artfully decorated, they stand among the finest objects of southern craftsmanship.

Adam and Eve are depicted in this block from a quilt made by a Georgia black woman; the full quilt is shown on page 169.

Tools of hearth and home. Colonization of the southern states grew at such a pace in the 17th and 18th Centuries that it was impossible for local craftsmen to keep up with the tremendous demand for household utensils, building hardware, tools, lamps, and heating equipment. Much material was imported, especially from England. But, increasingly, southern foundries – there were great ones in Virginia and Maryland – hammered out raw material, and recently emigrated blacksmiths and metalworkers converted it into useful artifacts. Black workmen were frequently trained in the craft and on plantations and in cities they became skilled masters. Much of the wrought iron of New Orleans was made by black artisans. Copper, brass and pewter objects were especially prized because of the relative scarcity and cost of the material. Precious pots and plates were carefully mended and re-used; in some cases they were melted down and recast in new forms, sometimes to conform to changing fashions. A 1792 advertisement from a Baltimore newspaper, placed by a recent immigrant from Holland, is revealing. The maker, a coppersmith, brassfounder and tinker named Samuel Beacher, asserts that "he makes Iron Stoves and Pipes, mends all Household Furniture of Copper and Brass . . . he mends Pewter Dishes, Plates and Basons [sic] and makes them as good as new. . . ." Regrettably Beacher's work, like that of most of his fellows, cannot be identified; the pieces are unmarked and their histories lost.

Placed before a fireplace, this simple iron oven with a spit was used to roast meat or fowl by radiant heat.

Necessary metals. In the early, and mostly rural South, improvements in the basic, age-old forms of indoor lighting were late in developing and mostly ineffective. As in England, wax candles and animal fat or whale oil served as fuel for lamps. Most homes had their own candlemolds, and housewives regularly poured or dipped a fresh supply of tapers. At the left are a group of candleholding devices: a two-candle sconce with a hammered tin reflecting back; a wall sconce with a canopy to keep the flame away from the wall; a tinned sheet iron chandelier; and a single candlestick with a movable slide by which an old candle stub can be ejected. This type of stick is known as a "hogscraper," because the sharp edge of the base was sometimes used as a kitchen tool for cleaning slaughtered animals and for scraping hides before dressing them. At the bottom of this page is a candlesnuffer of the scissors type; the burning end of the wick was neatly snipped off and deposited in the box. Below is a simple, early oil lamp, made of tin. The oil lamp and later the gas light were subsequently refined to a high degree for a clear, bright, smokeless illumination. But not until electricity was introduced in the South in Richmond in 1887 was easy and efficient domestic lighting a practical and safe convenience.

Southern colonists had somewhat less need of heating equipment than Northerners, but were certainly not wholly favored by climate. At Nomini Hall, the Virginia plantation of Robert Carter, the late January consumption of wood in 1774 was four cart loads a day to keep twenty-eight fires burning. Wood, of course, was the prime fuel and, in the English manner, the open fireplace was the rule. Andirons, below left, plus a few tools were the only equipment needed for a hearth fire; to protect the chimney base, a cast iron fireback was often placed against the brick back wall of the hearth. The fireback at left made by Isaac Zane of Marlboro, Virginia, is one of the most beautiful known. To make wood fires more efficient and stop the smoke that often accompanied fireplace heating, Benjamin Franklin and others tried inventing a cast iron fireplace that would draw smoke out of the room and add the potential heat of the hot iron to the total warmth available. The stove at left was cast at the Catoctin furnace in Maryland and is similar to Franklin's design which, though it gave its name to all such stoves, was never either popular or successful. At right is a later model of the familiar pot-bellied stove – used here to heat irons for laundering. Finally, with all early heating equipment there was a great danger of fire. In some cities, like Baltimore, private fire companies served subscribing households; the iron firemark above at left was hung beside the front door to signal membership in the protection scheme, a guarantee that the fire fighters would stop at the right house.

Foreign-made locks, hinges and hardware dominated the American market until long after the Revolution. But some local makers, primarily blacksmiths, hammered out the needed ironware, albeit in small quantities, as soon as their forges were hot. The two decorative hinges and "elbow" lock shown were made in the Moravian community at Salem, North Carolina, where it is clear that more than pure function animated the thoughts of the ironworker. Even more fanciful is the brass doorknob at left, also from Salem, and made by the silversmith John Vogler for his own shop. Some makers went so far as to sign their work. *Lower left:* The pewter sundial was made by a man with the appropriate name of Goldsmith Chandlee, from Winchester, Virginia, whose sundials of lead and other materials are also known. *Upper left:* Also proudly cut with the maker's name is the elegantly-shaped lock by C.J. Stewart of Baltimore; marked "Balto. Custom House," the lock was probably designed for that very building and especially made by Stewart.

In the very early years of the South, even the cleverest machine still relied on muscle-power liberally lubricated with elbow grease. The devices shown here are all southern and some are made with telltale yellow pine. *Upper left:* This is an apple peeler; the fruit was speared on the prong and the crank was turned – a blade attached to the long arm in front stripped the peeling off. *Lower left:* A cherry pitter was doubly efficient; at the end of the lever arm are two spears, right and left, so that each to and fro motion of the arm passed through the holder, at center, where a cherry was placed. The pits neatly rolled into the trough. *Left, below:* Here is a household broom-making machine. *Below:* Bait was placed on the thin board at the center of the frame of this mousetrap. When a mouse took the bait, the heavy board above fell down upon it. *Right:* This is a "shoo-fly chair," an ingenious rig whereby a person sitting at work could, with one foot, operate a swinging arm hung with rags to swish the air clear of buzzing pests.

145

Kitchen gear. Boasting of his daughters, William Byrd of Virginia wrote that "They are every day up to their elbows in housewifery which will qualify them effectually for useful wives, and if they live long enough, for notable women." And, indeed, even the offspring of a wealthy man like Byrd were required to learn the domestic arts, although they often had plenty of servants to assist them. Cooking, of course, was the chief chore of the colonial woman, and the tradition of good food in the South got an early start. At Jamestown in 1634, a guest found "tables fournished with porke, kidd, chickens, turkeys, young geese, Caponetts, and such other fouls ... besides plenty of milk, cheese, butter, and corne." In preparing her food for the table, the southern cook had access to a wide variety of implements, not unlike those shown in the well-stocked kitchen of a Salem, North Carolina tobacconist at left. Many kitchen tools were imported from England, but increasingly more were made in this country, although usually on an English or continental pattern. The metal cake mold and the coffee grinder follow a European design, as does the decorated rolling pin, though it was made in North Carolina. It is used for making the delicious German anise cookies called springerle. The Moravian silversmith, John Vogler, may have carved this one for his wife.

Durability was a prime requisite in early cooking utensils, but the weight of iron and steel pieces like these must have tested a housewife's strength with the preparation of every meal. *Left:* Here is a ten-gallon kettle of cast iron made in Baltimore. *Below:* This clever mechanical fork was used for removing baked potatoes from a fire. *Right:* A cast-iron kettle was fitted with a tilter by which the kettle could be tipped forward as it hung above a fire. *Below right:* A shapely tripod skillet made of bell metal – a type of bronze – bears the maker's name, John Taylor of Richmond, on its handle. *Far right:* The U-shaped blade of this steel tool was used to core apples; the reverse twist of the handles made turning the blade relatively effortless.

In materials, inventiveness and design, the kitchen tools of the pre-industrial South often seem more like art objects than purely functional things. *Above left:* These cowhorn spoons were probably whittled on the Louisiana plantation where they were used. *Below left:* This tinned sheet iron tool serves both as a funnel and a sieve. *Below:* A wooden lemon squeezer. *Left:* The ring-turned walnut handle of this S-blade chopper adds a decorative touch, but also makes the handle easier to grip.

Above right: The proud maker of this copper kettle stamped his name atop the three-lobed handle. He was George Reed, an Irish immigrant who settled in Winchester, Virginia, in 1788. A coppersmith by trade, Reed was also a Methodist minister, mayor of Winchester, a county magistrate, and high sheriff. *Right, below:* Stacked with slices of fresh-cut bread and thrust before an open fire, this wrought iron gadget served as a handy toaster; the top swivels so that both sides of the bread could be easily browned. *Far right:* Shaped like ram's horns, the curling ears of this wrought iron utensil were used to hang broiling skewers, each of which had a ring-eye.

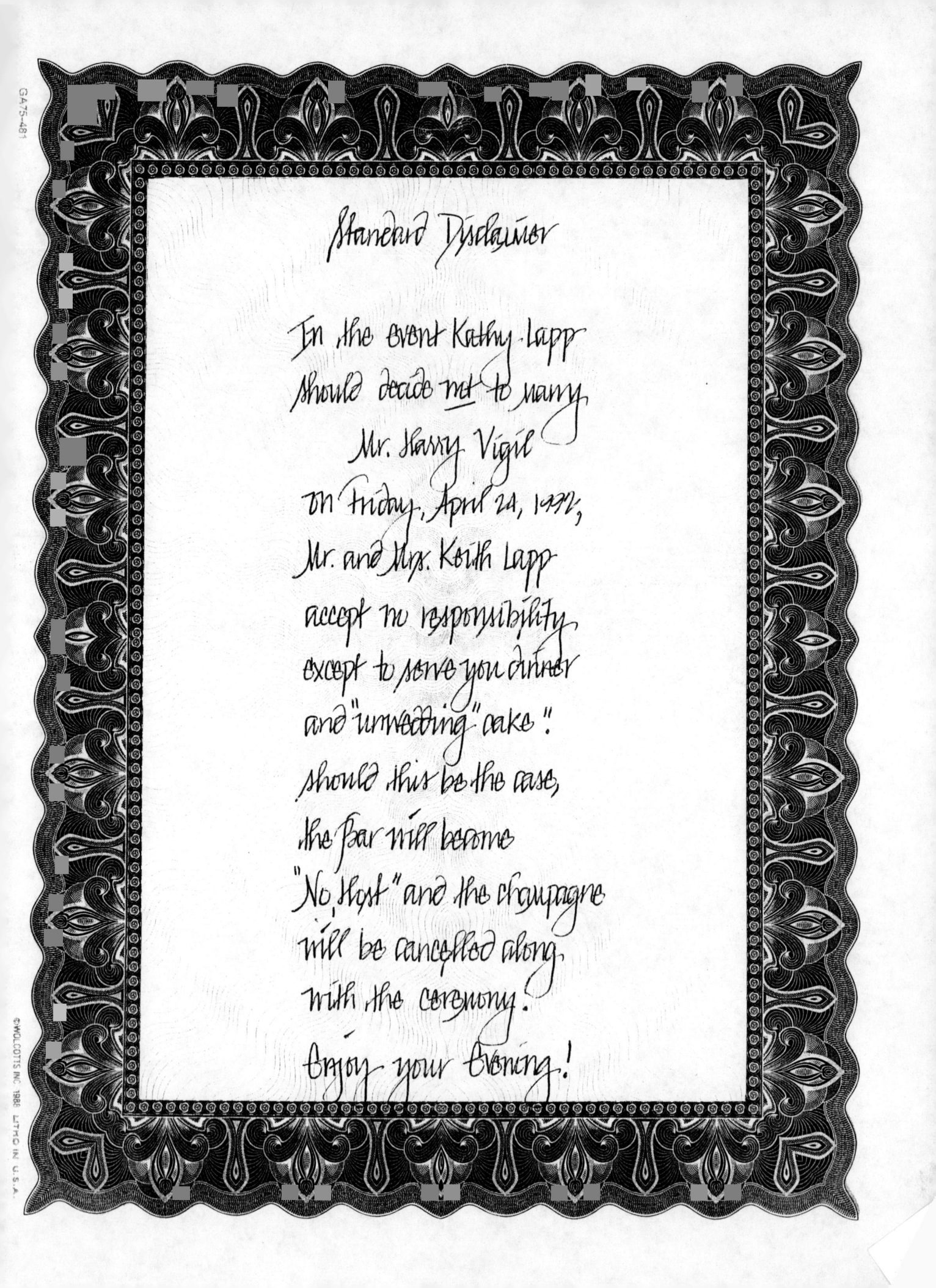

Standard Disclaimer

In the event Kathy Lapp
should decide not to marry
Mr. Harry Vigil
on Friday, April 24, 1992,
Mr. and Mrs. Keith Lapp
accept no responsibility,
except to serve you dinner
and "unwedding" cake".
should this be the case,
the bar will become
"No Host" and the champagne
will be cancelled along
with the ceremony.
Enjoy your evening!

Since glass and ceramic containers were in short supply – or relatively expensive – in early times, a great many receptacles were made of wood or leather. *Upper left:* A wooden pitcher, also called a noggin, was used not only to pour from but also as a kind of mug, passed around the table for drinking. *Lower left:* This handsome bowl was made from a walnut burl sliced from the tree and hollowed out; it has iron loop handles. *Left:* This elegant tooled leather basket may have been made by an imprisoned slave in a Richmond penitentiary. *Left, below:* Oak sides and a yellow pine base make up this bucket.

Upper right: Straw and split hickory were used in this covered basket, probably made between 1850 and 1900. Woven of coils of straw and secured with bands of hickory, it is deftly tapered so the cover fits snugly. *Lower right:* Also made of split hickory, this basket with a handle is in the collections at Williamsburg.

Fabrics for living. Among the schooling received by proper young ladies in the early South was a complete course in needlework. A Virginia teacher in 1766 offered a curriculum that included "Petit Point in Flowers, Fruit, Landscapes, and Sculpture, Nuns Work, Embroidery in Silk, Gold, Silver, Pearls, or embossed, Shading of all kinds, in the various works in Vogue, Dresden Point Work, Lace Ditto . . . Painting in Water Colours and Mezzo Tinto; also the art of taking off Foliage, with Several other Embellishments for the Amusement of Persons of Fortune who have Taste." For girls of lesser "fortune," especially in the back country, needlework skills were a necessary component of daily life. The womanly work of sewing, weaving, dyeing and quilting furnished all the textile needs of the family. And despite the large amounts of time expended in taking the raw materials from a natural state, weaving the cloth, and then stitching it into useful articles – despite this labor, there was time for decoration. From simple samplers to elaborate and sophisticated needlework pictures, from beaded purses to candlewick bedspreads, and finally, in perhaps the grandest expression of decorative needlework – the pieced, appliquéd or patchwork quilt – the southern woman showed not only her skill but her artistic sense, her eye for color and her knowledge of and interest in the significant symbols of the life she lived.

Left: A Piedmont bedroom filled with local homespun. *Above:* A needlework cat set with glass bead eyes and mounted as a footstool.

Textile tools. A variety of tools, mostly derived from the long, well-established tradition of textile crafts in England and on the Continent, aided the southern back country housewife in making the family's linens and simple clothing. The familiar spinning wheel was a fixture in many homes; on it, cotton, wool, and flax were spun into thread to be woven or sewn. A yarn reel below served to take up the thread and also as a drying rack after dyeing. *Lower left:* The tape loom was used to weave tough, decorative bands of tightly braided fabric that were employed as fancy work on clothing and upholstery; some Shaker furniture contains woven bands of tape on seat bottoms and backs. *Left:* This spool holder of the late 19th Century provided not only an orderly place to store thread but a convenient pin cushion on top. A degree of mechanization was built into the yarn winder at far left. Click stops on the racheted center axle of the six-arm winder were preset for a fixed number of revolutions; at the desired number of turns, a bell inside the center post would ring, signifying that a known length of yarn had been received on the winder. The device was known as a "weasel," and the familiar popular song of the 1850s – "Pop Goes the Weasel" – probably was derived from this gadget.

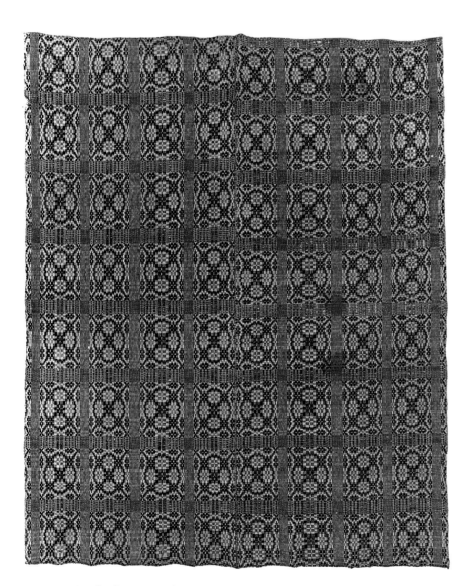

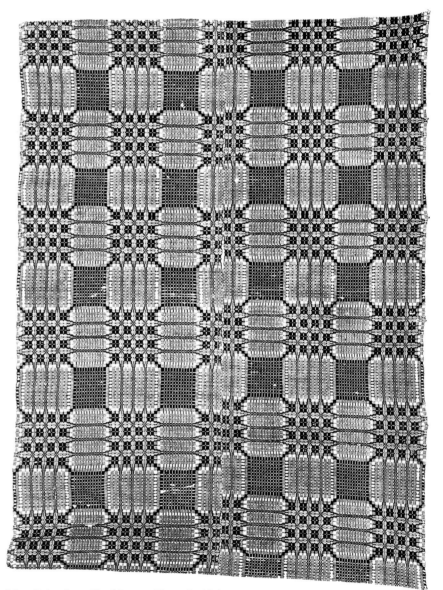

The simplest bed covers, often woven at home on small looms, were overshot coverlets made with a warp (lengthwise threads) of linen crossed by a woof of dyed wool. This Virginia coverlet of about 1815 is done in the "Lace and Compass" pattern.

Mrs. John Lovell of Jones Chapel, Alabama, wove this overshot coverlet with wool produced and dyed on the family farm in about 1888. She used a pattern called "Pine Bloom," stitching several widths together for a full-sized coverlet.

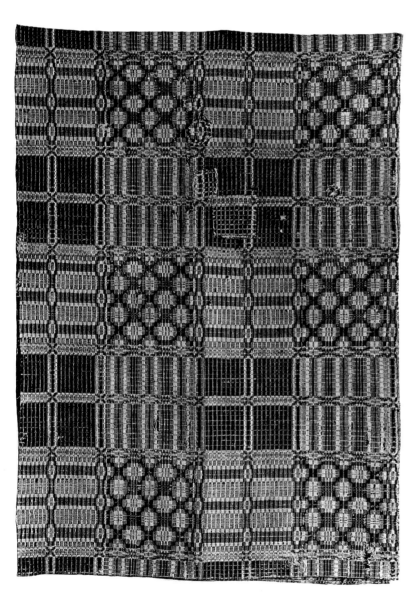

Well over three hundred known patterns were woven in the three basic types of coverlets, called overshot, double-weave, and summer and winter. This unusual one is called "Tennessee Trouble," perhaps referring to a threatened bankruptcy of the state.

In 1820, a new weaving device invented by a Frenchman, Joseph Jacquard, swept America. Using a punched card like a piano roll, the adaptation produced complex patterns on ordinary looms. This coverlet depicts West Virginia's short-lived Hemfield Railroad.

Needlework crafts. Both plain and fancy needlework was done by girls at home and at the growing number of boarding schools in the South, where young ladies were taught the useful and social graces. The first test of a girl's skill was a sampler, a decorative panel usually about twenty-four inches across, on which were stitched both pictorial elements and alphabets in upper and lower case letters with numerals. In addition, the girl usually added some form of inscription with her name, the date, and the school or place where she lived. The function was not only to show that the student had mastered a repertoire of embroidery stitches, but that she knew her alphabet and numbers as well. Also, by copying an inscription from the Bible or some elevating work of literature, she adeptly demonstrated her reading ability. Few more complete and satisfying schoolwork exercises have ever been devised. As girls increased their competence, they not only did more elaborate samplers, but went on to turn out other, more complicated needlework forms. One elaborate project may have involved stitching a beaded purse like those shown here; the black silk bag below, with beads of black, white, and shades of blue, was made by a student at the Salem Academy around 1825. The fancier bag at the left, also made at Salem, is shown open and closed.

Needlework pictures were extremely popular in the 19th Century. Done with exquisite skill, often in silk thread on a silk or satin base, the pictures tend to follow certain formulas — but also usually show individuality as well. The scene below depicts a courting couple. Some subjects were done in a variety of mediums. The scene of Ruth and Naomi at upper left, for example, was a popular motif for so-called theorem paintings, watercolors done on velvet. A new technique called Berlin work — essentially needlepoint stitched on canvas, often to a pre-printed pattern — took hold in America at about the middle of the century and largely superceded earlier forms of ornamental work. The technique, used in the charming picture at lower left, is still much in vogue. Missing from today's needlework, however, is the sentiment revealed in mourning pictures such as that at right. This moving scene commemorated the death of a seventeen-year old boy and was done by one of his devoted sisters. Here, some painting has been added to the embroidery and a verse is written in ink on paper and glued to the silk background.

Slow waves the Willow
That points o'er the Stone,
where sleeps a Brother dear,
Oft have I sought
the spot alone
To shew at ease
the solitary tear.

C.A.N.
1826

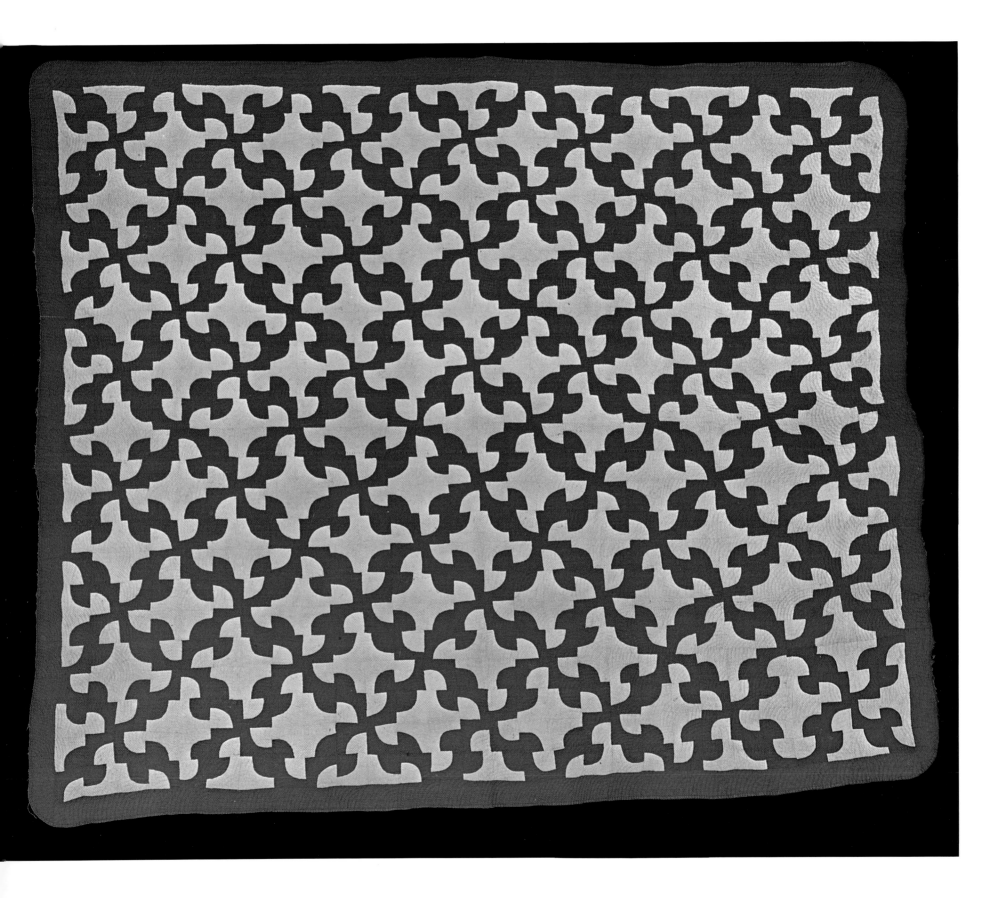

164

Quilts and coverlets. The enormous variety of quilt designs would be virtually impossible to catalog, but basically there are two techniques for making them: the patchwork or pieced quilt, and the appliqué. Interestingly, both techniques economically rely on recycling old or worn fabrics – clothing, bed linens, or commercial textiles. The two quilts shown on these pages are of the appliqué type; the decorative elements have been cut out of fabrics, sometimes sewn together, and then stitched onto the background. *Left:* This design was made in Kentucky in 1860 and is called Drunkard's Path. *Below:* This 1840 quilt commemorates the Presidential campaign of William Henry Harrison, whose symbols were the log cabin and cider barrel.

This delicate white-on-white coverlet was worked in Kentucky sometime before 1810. Employing both embroidery and drawnwork, the coverlet shows a floral design popular fifty years earlier. It also indicates the long continuity of needlework designs and techniques, since drawnwork of this kind is known from ancient Egypt.

From Frederick, Maryland, this embroidered candlewick bedspread illustrates a technique in which twisted cotton cording resembling the wicks of candles is used to form a kind of "pile" like that in a carpet. Usually made in white-on-white, candlewick spreads were also done in white and a second color.

Eschewing a traditional or geometric pattern, Virginia Ivey stitched into an 1856 counterpane a representation of the fairgrounds near Russellville, Kentucky. In this detail, the charming scene is filled with horses and other animals and shows the arena.

Poverty need not handicap the artistic spirit. *Right:* This wonderfully imaginative quilt was made by Harriet Powers, a black woman born in the age of slavery. Mrs. Powers exhibited it at the Athens, Georgia Cotton Fair of 1886, and was asked to sell it. She refused to part with it for any price. But four years later, badly needing the money, she agreed to sell it – for five dollars. Today it holds an honored place among national treasures at the Smithsonian Institution in Washington. (Another Powers Bible quilt is at the Boston Museum of Fine Arts.) Mrs. Powers knew her Bible well; here is the story of Adam and Eve in the Garden of Eden, Adam naming the animals, Cain's slaying of Abel, Jacob's dream, the baptism, betrayal and crucifixion of Christ, the Last Supper, and a history of the Holy Family. Made entirely of cotton, the quilt is mostly handsewn but shows some machine stitching in the appliqué; it is lined with cotton wadding. A detail of the Bible quilt appears on page 135. *Left:* Similar in spirit is this decorative appliqué and pieced work quilt showing the "firmament" in the center and around the heavenly circle a sequence of scenes in the life of Adam and Eve: Adam is shown in the Garden of Eden, Eve is seen taking the apple and the couple are depicted in flight after their expulsion. Made at or near Fort Smith, Arkansas about 1900, the quilt is a charming, naive piece of work.

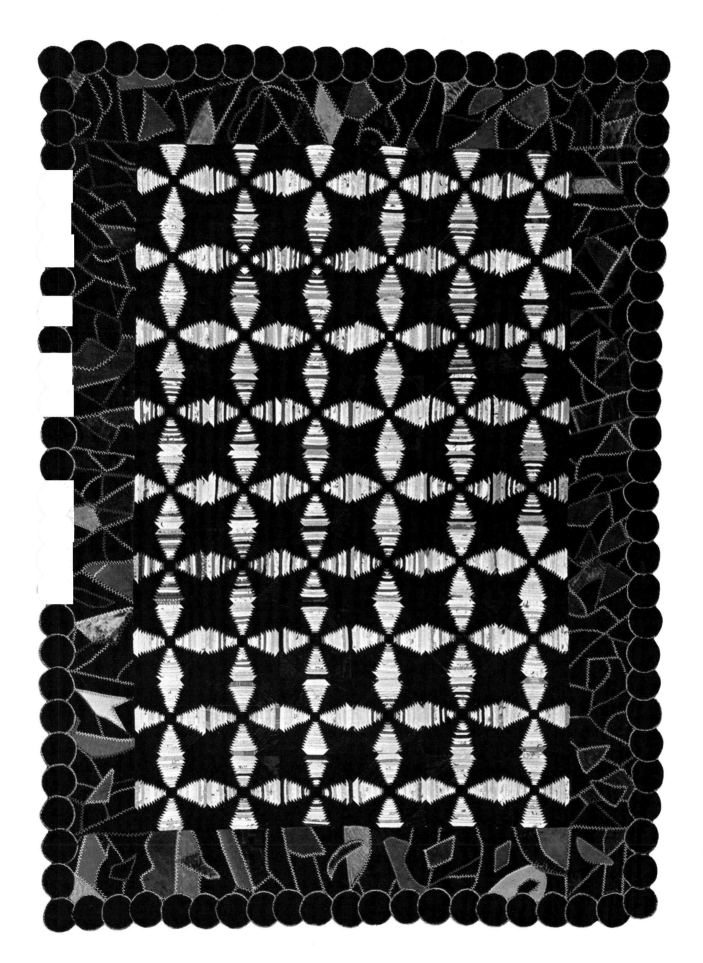

Velvet, satin, silk and taffeta make up this fancy pieced throw from Texas. Intended for show and probably displayed in a parlor, the piece is not actually quilted, although the border resembles that of a "crazy quilt." It won first prize at a San Antonio fair in 1906.

This delightful appliquéd, woolen
counterpane was made about 1900 by a young
lady who could hardly have come from
anywhere but Virginia: her name –
Pocahontas Virginia Gay. Slightly under six
feet square, the throw was probably used as a
decorative piece rather than as a bed cover.

Some quilts can be read like a book, and this dazzling example, now at Mobile, relates the story of a family's interests. It is made up of silk lapel badges from a variety of organizations: mainly Confederate group reunions, railroad conventions (a clue to the father's occupation), and political campaigns. Just under eight feet square and backed in red cotton, the quilt was made in 1897; the date is embroidered at center.

172

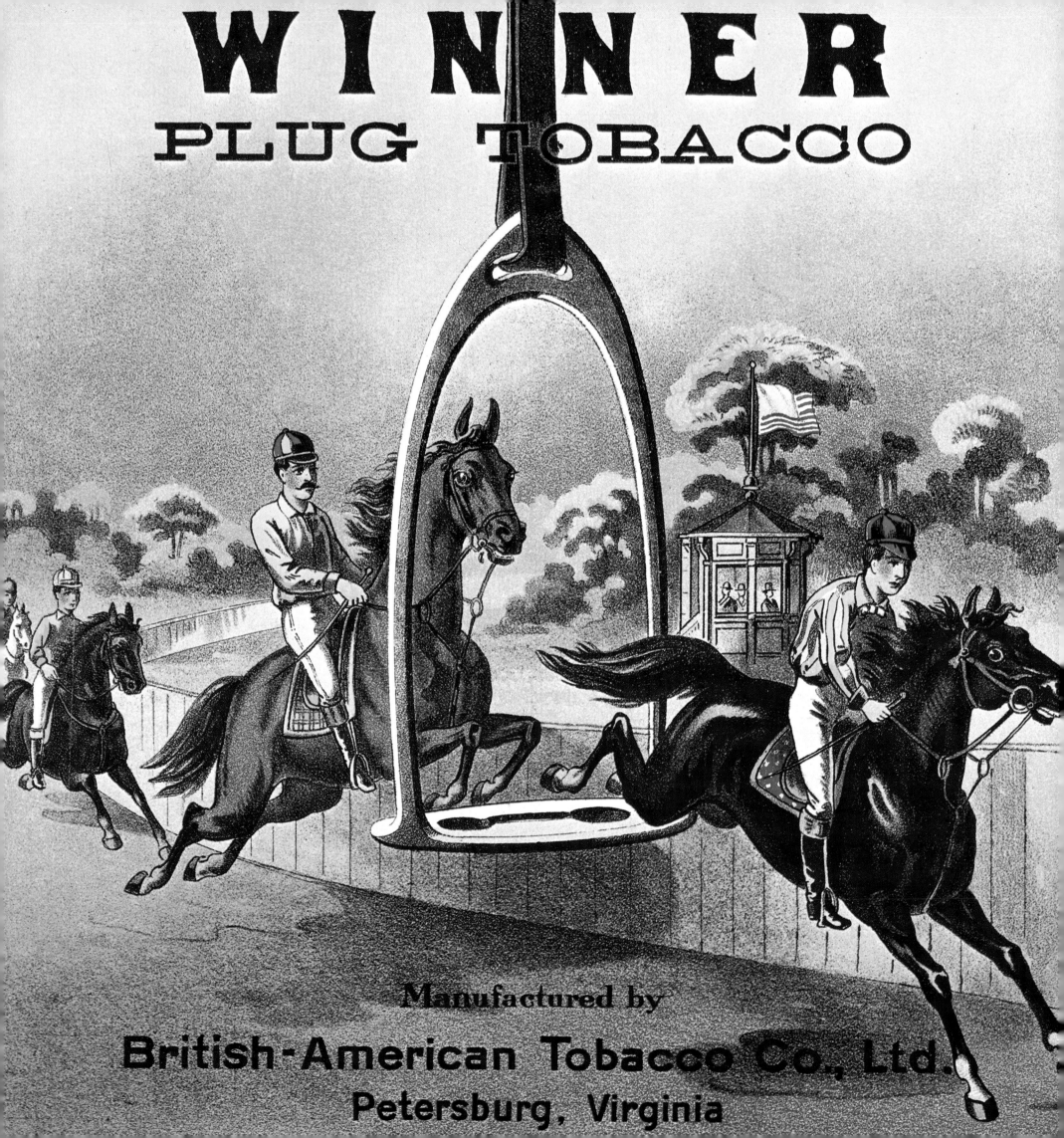

Advertising and trade. Artifacts from the world of commerce and industry, trade and the professions have become increasingly valuable, not only as collectors' items, but as revelations of the style and art of business in the past. Although the South was largely agricultural for many of its early years, there was no shortage of commercial and advertising ephemera produced. Few of the objects had any intrinsic value and since most were quickly and cheaply made, the great bulk of them have disappeared. But durable and beautiful ones remain. Chief among the products of the South were tobacco and cotton, although cotton was produced essentially as a raw material and shipped abroad or to the north to industrial manufacturing centers. Tobacco, however, still a prime industry in the South, was prepared for consumer use, and the advertising and packaging of the leaf generated a huge mass of printed and fabricated artifacts. Plug tobacco, along with snuff, accounted for the chief use of the product until quite late in the 19th Century when the cigarette became fashionable. In 1886, Allen and Ginter, one of the first cigarette makers in the South, were still rolling them by hand but had already introduced merchandising schemes – such as packets of cards with portraits of celebrities or sports figures – which were to help make cigarette smoking a national addiction. Oddly enough, the most dramatic form of tobacco advertising – the cigar store Indian used as a shop sign by tobacconists – seems to have taken little hold in the South.

Colorful posters and trade cards were used to advertise plug tobacco and cigarettes in the late 19th Century.

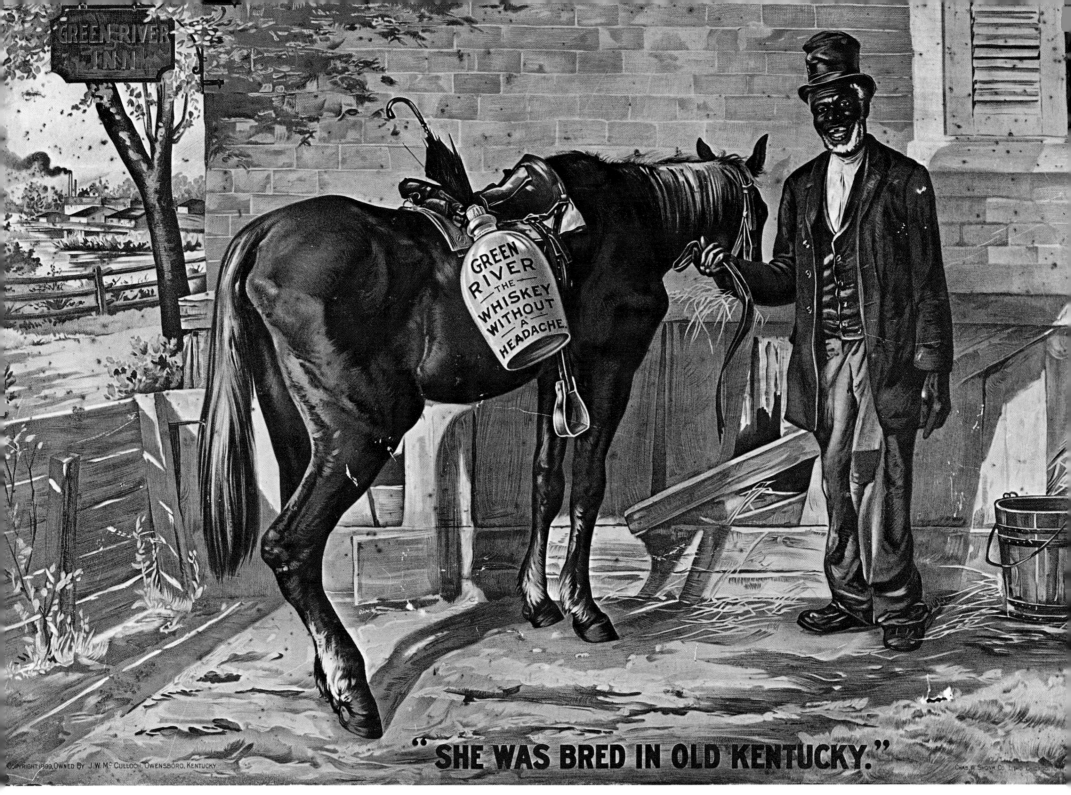

"SHE WAS BRED IN OLD KENTUCKY."

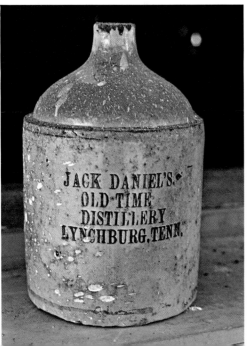

Bourbon whiskey has been manufactured and marketed in the South since the 1860s. The Jack Daniel Distillery, which produces bourbon by the sour mash method, was founded in 1866, making it the oldest registered distillery in this country. Before 1895, when the now familiar square glass bottle was introduced, Jack Daniel's whiskey was put up in a variety of containers, including ceramic jugs like the one at left. Homeowners decanted it for table use. Late in the 19th Century, colorful posters, above, brought new sparkle to whiskey advertising.

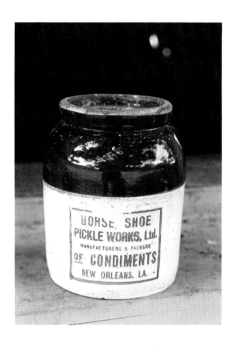

Before 1900, most products were put out in what today would be called "super-giant economy packages." Take, for example, the tins and jugs above – all attractive, efficient containers for what could be a six-months' supply. The disadvantage of such packaging, of course, was that part of the contents could become stale or moldy. In use well into the 20th Century, the durable containers have recently become quite valuable as collectors' items and numerous guide books to their identification and prices have been published. One of the few southern cigar store Indians known, this squaw was made and used in Louisiana. Research for this book turned up only this single example.

Social historians of the future may reach some
significant conclusion about the fact that
three of the four most popular American soda
pops were invented below the Mason-Dixon
line. Dr. Pepper, second oldest American soda
beverage (the oldest was Hire's Root Beer,
introduced at the Philadelphia Centennial
Exhibition in 1876) came on the market in
Waco, Texas, in 1885. It was the creation of a
former pharmacist's assistant from Virginia
who named the drink after his old boss.
Advertising and distribution were the keys to
its success, and by 1900, Dr. Pepper was
putting out attractive posters — emphasizing
youth, beauty, and a glowing healthfulness —
and hand-painted metal serving plates.

When an Atlanta druggist put Coca-Cola on sale in 1886 he started a world wide revolution in taste. First sold as an invigorating, exhilarating drink, "Coke" was claimed to relieve mental and physical exhaustion and cure headaches. In the course of Coca-Cola's advertising, millions of home and fountain artifacts — syrup dispensers, Tiffany-type lamps, serving trays, coupons, posters, and containers and packages (perhaps the most distinctive of which is the bottle itself) — have been produced. And in recent years, some of these early items have become collectors' pieces; the ad featuring turn-of-the-century opera star Lillian Norton Nordica is one of the most valuable.

179

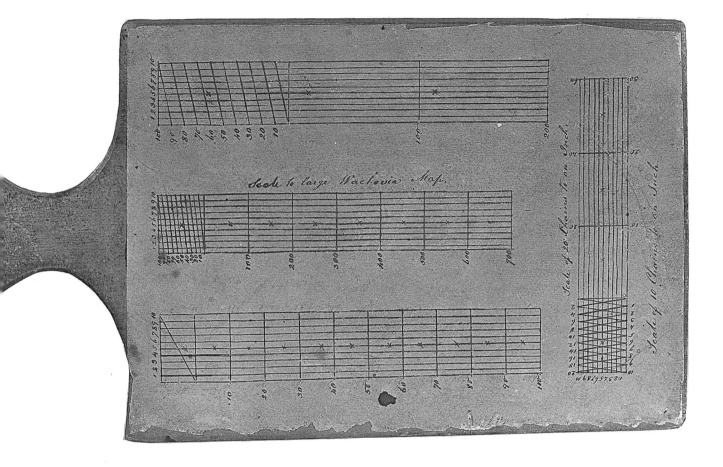

Tools of a trade are valued today not only for their historical interest but as evidence of a craftsman's skill. For most early professional tools — mathematical instruments, architects' and surveyors' equipment, medical implements, and measuring devices — were made by hand. At the left are a surveyor's compass and an architect's map scale; both were made and used in the Moravian community at Salem, North Carolina, a town hewn out of the woods by a mere handful of men and women beginning in 1766. Six years later, using such simple tools as these, they had laid out a full-scale village. Interestingly, the compass was made by John Vogler — by now a familiar name in this book — who also made the handsomely crafted veterinarian's instrument at lower right. Called a fleam, it is a spring-loaded mechanical lancet used for bleeding animals. Above it and its leather case is another fleam, made by a man who proudly announces himself as a "mathematical instrument maker," a rare profession in the early South. Rare too, is the barometer inscribed "Made and Sold by Bennett," a New Orleans craftsman. Often such devices were imported from abroad and stamped with a local purveyor's imprint; Bennett, however, seems to have crafted his products himself.

Many artifacts of business and the retail trade lend character to our view of the South's commercial past. Below is a case of eyeglass lenses sold by a Charleston dealer, who actually ran an all-purpose jewelry shop. Before the days of prescription lenses, pre-ground glass of varying strengths was sold for eyeglasses; the customer selected the ones that aided his vision the most. *Lower left:* Here is an older pair of spectacles, dating from 1820 to 1850, with frames crafted in brass; silver was also used. *Left:* This cotton stencil was used to mark the 400-pound bales that were packed on the plantation. *Right:* Here is a group of signs, the most interesting of which are a fish market sign from Louisiana and a Texas tinsmith's handmade shop marker, appropriately emblazoned with the Lone Star state's familiar symbol.

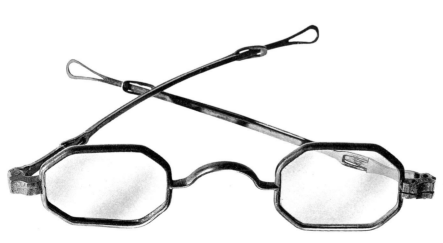

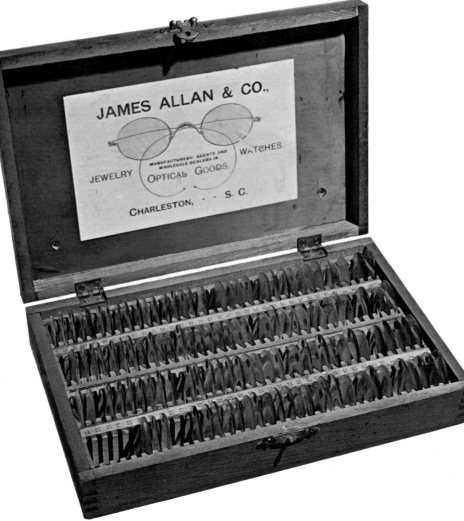

183

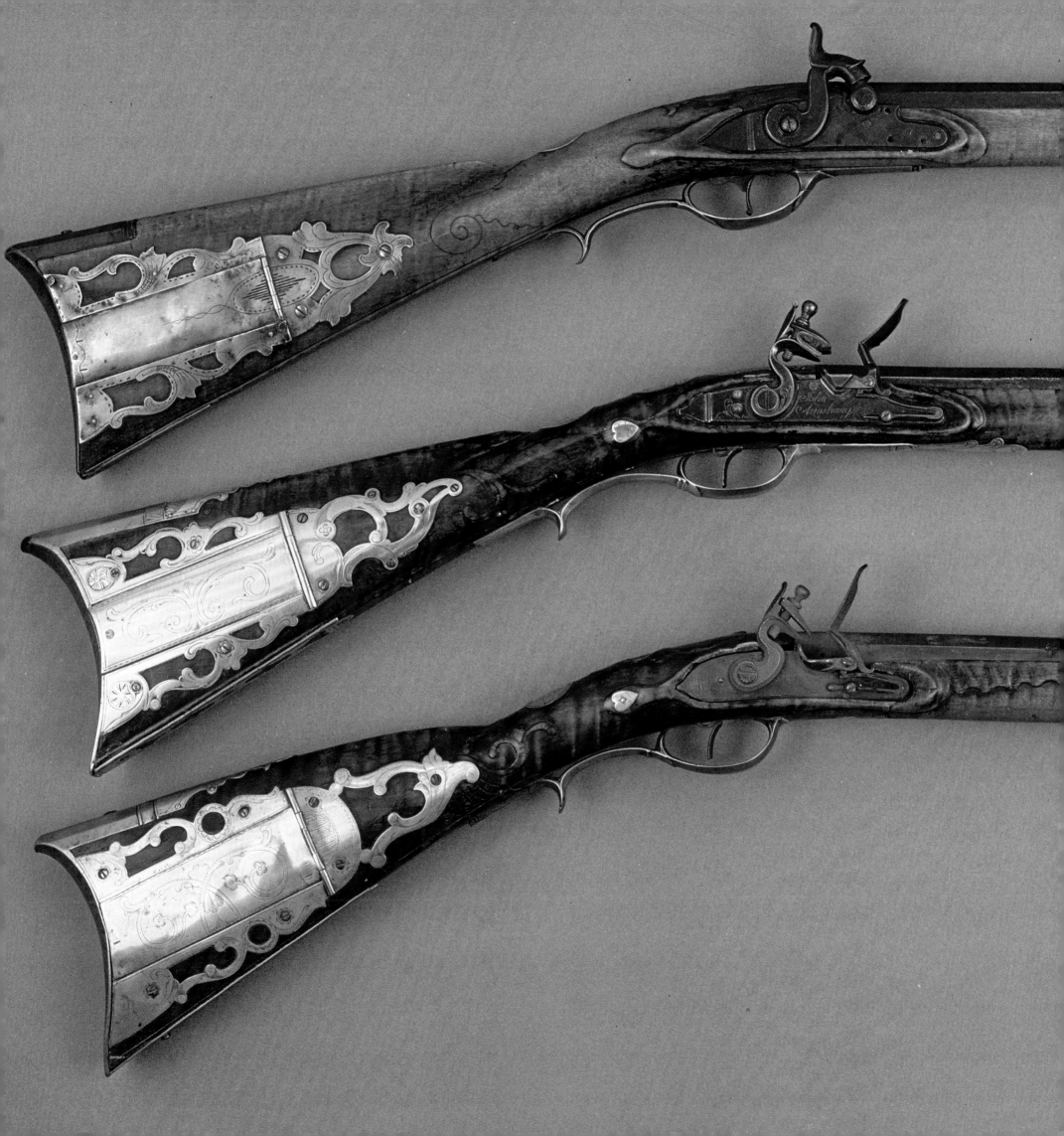

Hunting and military life. Guns, powder horns, bird decoys, flags and military paraphernalia fall just as naturally into a book on southern antiques as quilts and kettles. Guns, in particular, were part of the household equipment of every early rural family. Men and women alike were adept in their use: they shot meat for the table, brought back furs for clothing (and to trade or sell to British merchants) and defended themselves against marauding Indians and wandering outlaws. As the need for guns grew less, however, with the advance of the frontier farther westward, rifles and shotguns were employed for sport or casual shooting. During the Revolution, of course, and again at the end of the first decade of the 19th Century, the South was engaged in fighting against the British. Then, finally, in 1860 came the War Between the States. Civil War artifacts run a wide range – from weapons and uniforms to patriotic sheet music, souvenirs and printed memorabilia. Confederate currency and loan agreements have found a large collectors' market and, as much as anything, they speak of the past. Many different kinds of Civil War objects remain in private and public collections. The Museum of the Confederacy in Richmond, and many local historical societies and city museums contain quantities of fascinating material. Much of it has never been studied carefully, however, for like early furniture a few decades ago, it has not seemed worth the trouble.

Left: The stocks of three Maryland longrifles. *Above:* Souvenir of the Civil War: a portrait of Robert Hart, 55th Tennessee Infantry.

Armed with a long rifle, supplied by a powder horn and with cloth wadding and lead balls carried in a pocket or belt, the southern hunter provided food for his family, killed fur-bearing animals for trade, defended his home, and fought for his country. This rifle, marked LMB, was made in Rowan County, North Carolina, about 1810; its carved curly maple stock and vigorously engraved patchbox identify it as a product of the central Piedmont. The top powder horn, from the Cape Fear region of North Carolina, bears a stylized mermaid, and on the other side, the maker's name and the date, March 18, 1807. Beneath it is an earlier horn, dating from 1763 and evidently owned by Isham Davis of Albermarle County, Virginia, who fought in Havana, Cuba, in service to the British fleet. The bird decoys date mostly from the 19th Century. At left is a Watch Gander Swan from North Carolina; below are two Canada geese from Louisiana; at the right is a more modern Sickle-Billed Curlew decoy of a type made and used in Cape Charles, Virginia.

Artifacts of war: Of the many hundreds of private gunsmiths in the South before the Civil War – who worked in shops very like the Salem, North Carolina reconstruction shown at left – nearly all turned out arms for the Confederate cause after 1861. Sometimes they made rifles on archaic patterns simply because guns of any kind were so desperately needed. Even silversmiths, like James Conning of Mobile, Alabama, turned to the production of military equipment. *Left:* This is the hilt of a cavalry sword made by Conning in 1862. Actually, records show that Conning had sold military swords, buttons, gold braid, hats, plumes, and pistols during the Mexican War of 1845, but he may have only begun manufacturing them himself in 1861, when he engaged a swordmaker from Mississippi to set up a full-scale shop. In addition to cavalry swords, he made artillery sabres and swords for foot, field, and staff officers. Most Confederate weapons, however, were turned out by large-scale armories, and every seceding state except Florida produced firearms. The largest maker was Virginia, where a large Federal armory at Harper's Ferry had been in operation for many years; at the outbreak of the war, most of the operable machinery and thousands of guns were moved from Harper's Ferry to a safer Confederate site in Richmond.

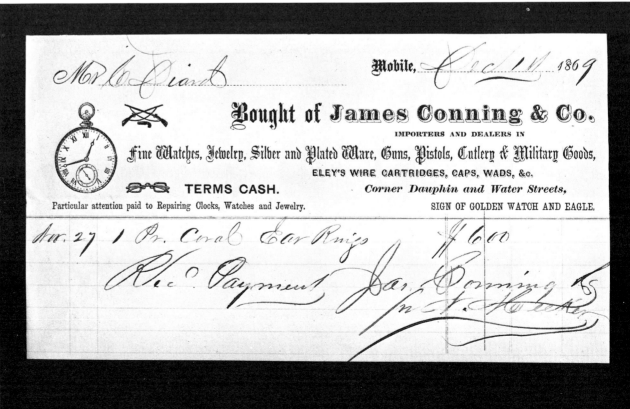

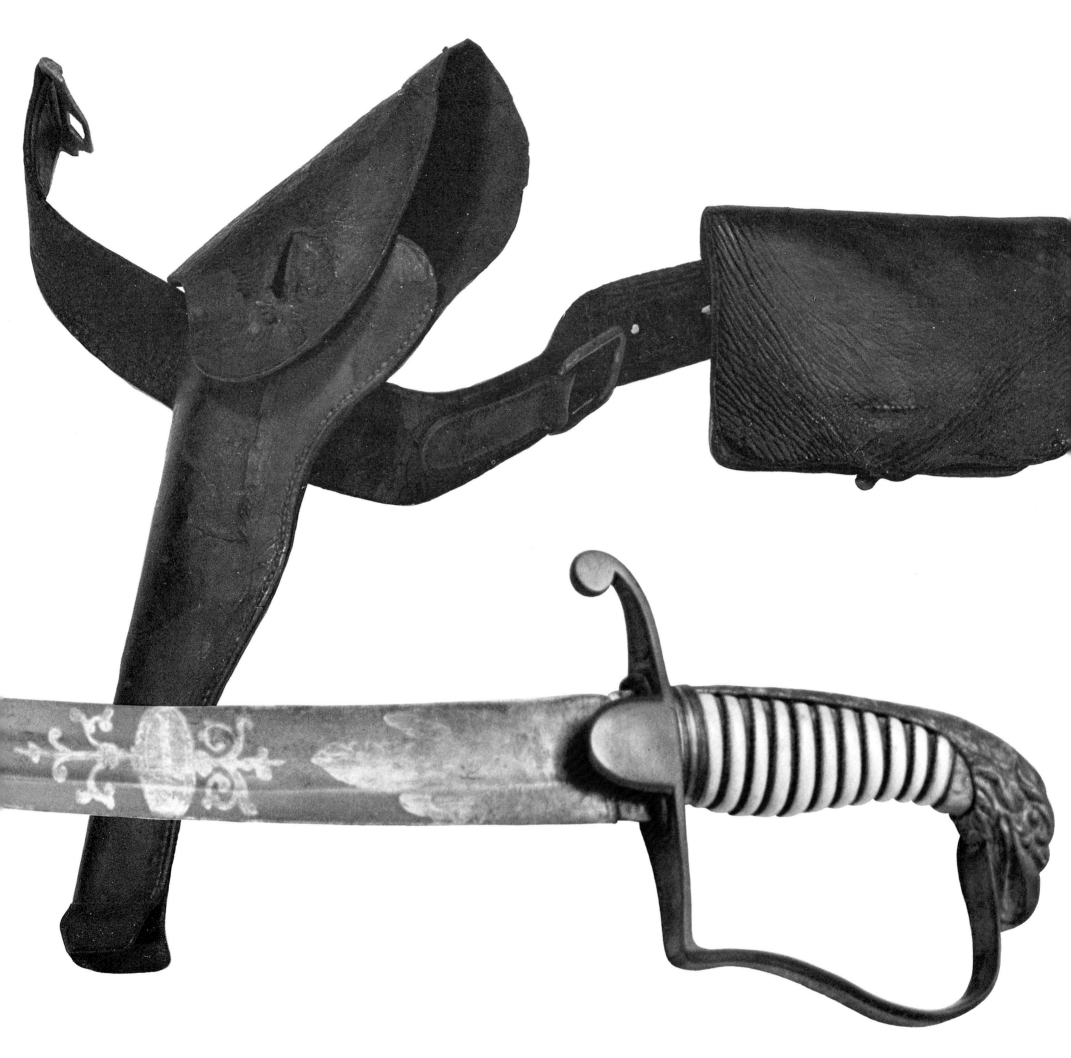

One of the most highly prized relics of the Civil War is the .36 caliber brass-framed revolver – a copy of the famous Colt. This one was made by Samuel Griswold of Griswoldville, Georgia, a town near Macon. It is shown with its belt, holster, and cartridge case. Before the war, Griswold had been in the business of making cotton gins, but he did his patriotic duty. In a similar conversion from peacetime to wartime activity – and in direct defiance of the Biblical injunction – the Nashville Plow Works turned to making swords. *Right:* This Nashville sword was carried by a colonel of the 41st Regiment of the Tennessee Volunteer Infantry. Many older weapons were unsheathed in the southern cause, but the sword at left, made by Clark and Rogers of New Orleans, was *hors de combat* by 1861. Used in battle against the British in 1813, it had already entered a museum collection by 1858.

192

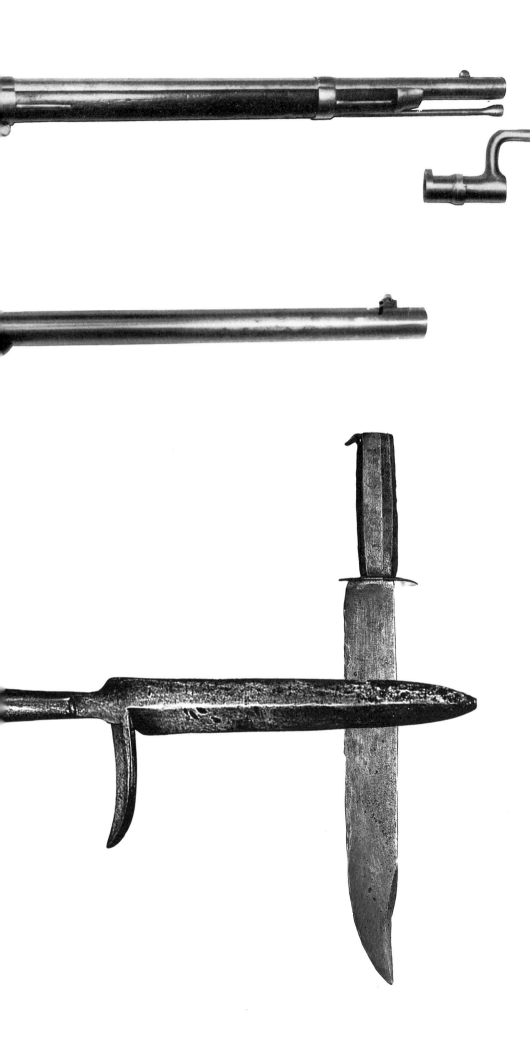

Perhaps the most effective of what specialists call "edged weapons" was the Bowie knife, named for James Bowie, the Georgia boy who worked and fought throughout the South and earned his fame at the Battle of the Alamo, where he was killed in 1836. The knife (it may have been invented by Bowie's brother Rezin) was adopted by various Confederate units; the open guard Bowie knife shown here with a brass plate on its handle is inscribed "Louisiana Tigers – Manassas 1861." Among some users, the Bowie knife was known as an Arkansas toothpick.

Given the shortage of conventional weapons in the Confederacy, it may not be surprising that someone came up with the medieval-looking pike shown at left. It was made in Georgia in 1862 for the notorious "Joe Brown" militia. Made in six- and eight-foot lengths, the pike had a side hook designed to snare a cavalryman's reins.

Above: The rifle with bayonet is a Richmond rifle musket, copied from an 1885 model gun made at Harper's Ferry. Rifled muskets could be loaded and fired three times a minute, and could hit a six-foot square target at 500 yards and an eight-footer at 1,000 yards about fifty percent of the time – an unusual degree of accuracy for a muzzle loader.

Rifles and carbines designed by Christian Sharps were used by both sides during the Civil War. The breech-loading model of 1863 had a coffee mill fitted into its stock so that a foraging infantryman might grind up some corn, grain, or coffee beans.

SEVEN PER CENT · FEBRUARY 20 1863.

Confederate States of America
LOAN,

Authorized by the Act of Congress · C.S.A. of February 20th 1863.

Nº. $1000 $1000 Nº.
8942 8942

On the first day of July 1868, the Confederate States of America, will pay to the Bearer of this Bond, at the seat of Government, or at such place of deposit as may be appointed by the Secretary of the Treasury, the Sum of **ONE THOUSAND DOLLARS**, with Interest thereon from date, at the rate of Seven per Cent per annum, payable semi annually, on the surrender of the annexed Coupons. This Contract is authorized by An Act of Congress approved 20th February 1863, Entitled "An Act to Authorize the issue of Bonds for funding Treasury Notes, and is upon the Express Condition that said Confederate States, may from time to time, extend the time of payment, for any period not exceeding thirty years, from this date, at the same rate of interest, upon the surrender of the Bond.

In Witness Whereof, the Register of the Treasury, in pursuance of said Act of Congress hath hereunto set his hand and affixed the Seal of the Treasury at Richmond, this second day of March 1863.

SEVEN PER CENT
Entered
Recorded

SEVEN PER CENT

Register of the Treasury

C.S. Loan Feby. 20th 1863.	C.S. Loan Feby. 20th 1863.	C.S. Loan Feby. 20th 1863.	C.S. Loan Feby. 20th 1863.
THE CONFEDERATE STATES of AMERICA WILL PAY TO BEARER THIRTY-FIVE DOLLARS for Six Months Interest, due July 1st 1868 on Bond Nº 8942 for $1000. for Regr of Treasr	THE CONFEDERATE STATES of AMERICA WILL PAY TO BEARER THIRTY-FIVE DOLLARS for Six Months Interest, due Jany 1st 1868 on Bond Nº 8942 for $1000. for Regr of Treasr	THE CONFEDERATE STATES of AMERICA WILL PAY TO BEARER THIRTY-FIVE DOLLARS for Six Months Interest, due July 1st 1867 on Bond Nº 8942 for $1000. for Regr of Treasr	THE CONFEDERATE STATES of AMERICA WILL PAY TO BEARER THIRTY-FIVE DOLLARS for Six Months Interest, due Jany 1st 1867 on Bond Nº 8942 for $1000. for Regr of Treasr
C.S. Loan Feby. 20th 1863.	C.S. Loan Feby. 20th 1863.	C.S. Loan Feby. 20th 1863.	
THE CONFEDERATE STATES of AMERICA WILL PAY TO BEARER THIRTY-FIVE DOLLARS for Six Months Interest, due July 1st 1866 on Bond Nº 8942 for $1000. for Regr of Treasr	THE CONFEDERATE STATES of AMERICA WILL PAY TO BEARER THIRTY-FIVE DOLLARS for Six Months Interest, due Jany 1st 1866 on Bond Nº 8942 for $1000. for Regr of Treasr	THE CONFEDERATE STATES of AMERICA WILL PAY TO BEARER THIRTY-FIVE DOLLARS for Six Months Interest, due July 1st 1865 on Bond Nº 8942 for $1000. for Regr of Treasr	

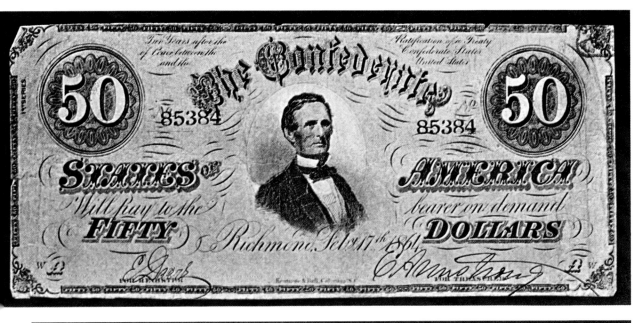

Although Confederate money was rendered worthless by the Federal Government at the end of the Civil War, the surviving paper bills have become collectors' items. Metal was so precious in the Confederacy that no coins were minted, but notes in values as low as fifty cents were issued, as well as large denominational bonds that were to have paid seven percent interest over five years. A charming attitude toward Confederate money was revealed in the words of a former major in the rebel army who inscribed the following verses on a note as a souvenir for a northern girl visiting in Virginia:

We knew it was hardly a value in gold,
Yet as gold each soldier received it;
It gazed in our eyes with a promise to pay,
And each Southern patriot believed it.

But our boys thought little of price or of pay
Or of bills that were overdue;
We knew that it brought us our bread today,
'Twas the best our poor country could do.

Artifacts of the war years run a wide gamut — buttons, belt buckles, and other insignia identifying Confederate army and navy regiments. The two buckles at the right are variations of standard issue types; one is called tongue-in-wreath, the other is a rectangular CSA. *Left:* This small, green silk flag was used by a Tennessee regiment commanded by a proud Irishman. *Lower right:* The famous form of the Confederate uniform cap, with the flat top sloping toward the front and a visor, is called a kepi. This one belonged to Captain G. Gaston Otey.

Here are two distinctive souvenirs of the war. *Right:* This printed proclamation was issued in protest against an order by the officer in charge of the northern forces occupying New Orleans. The Union General declared that demonstrations of abuse will be met by behavior from the troops such as would be fitting for prostitutes. The insult resulted in this proclamation by the men of New Orleans calling for revenge. A milder patriotic action was taken by William Aiken Walker, a celebrated painter of southern life, who created this deck of cards.

PRESIDENT DAVIS.

W. A. Walker.

CHARLESTON.S.C. SEP. 1864.

GEN. STONEWALL JACKSON.

197

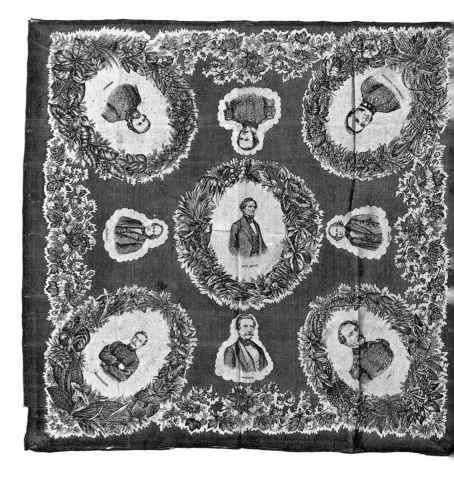

Songs and sheet music bolstered the patriotic spirit of the South during the war years. *Left:* This title page is from a rousing tune printed in Nashville. *Below:* Another souvenir is a cotton kerchief printed in London, which bears portraits of Confederate leaders and war heroes. One of the tenderest mementoes of the War, however, is the locket shown here, containing a piece of the apple tree under which Lee made the final surrender of the war. A report of the events of the surrender indicates that the apple tree under which Lee waited for the ceremonies to conclude was cut to pieces and carried away, roots included, by Confederate troops before the day was over. *Right:* This title page of a history of the southern cause, printed in Kentucky about thirty years after the fighting ceased, is only one example of the mass of histories and memoirs that documented the awful struggle that ripped America.

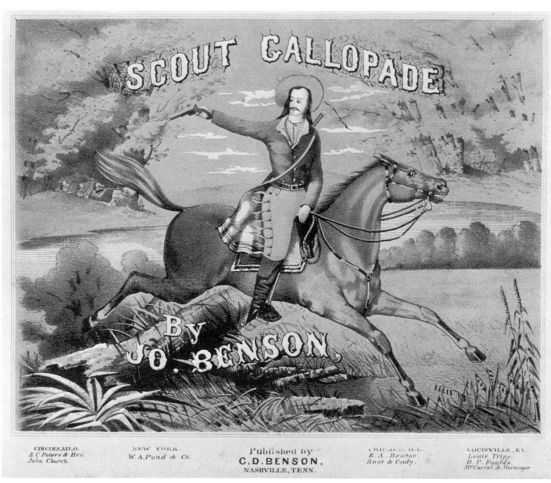

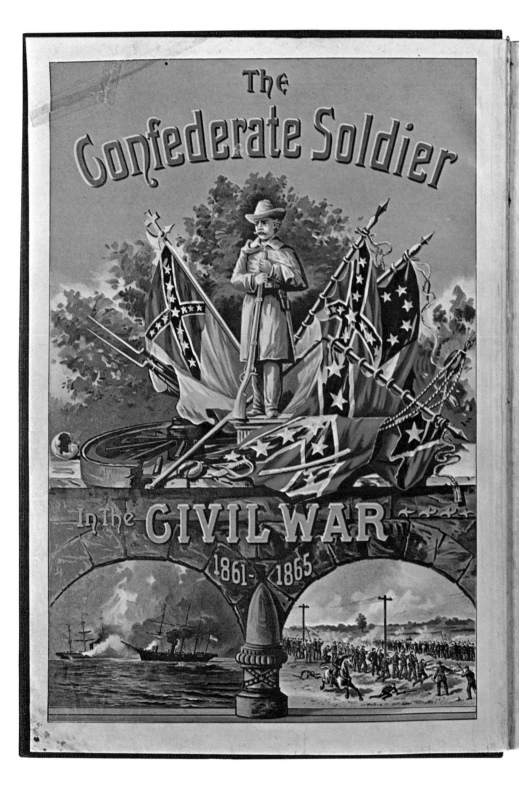

THE

CONFEDERATE SOLDIER

IN THE

CIVIL WAR

1861   1865

PREFACED BY A EULOGY BY

MAJOR-GENERAL FITZHUGH LEE,

Ex-Governor of Virginia, Commander of the Cavalry Corps, Army of Northern Virginia, Etc.

THE FOUNDATION AND FORMATION OF THE CONFEDERACY

AND THE SECESSION OF THE SOUTHERN STATES AND THE PROMINENT PARTS TAKEN

By HON. JEFFERSON DAVIS, President of the Confederate States;

Hon. ALEXANDER H. STEPHENS, Vice-President; Hons. JUDAH P. BENJAMIN, ROBERT TOOMBS, CHAS. G. MEMINGER, T. H. WATTS, GEO. A. TRENHOLM and LE ROY P. WALKER, Members of Cabinet; and Governors MOORE, of Alabama; RECTOR, of Arkansas; PERRY, of Florida; BROWN, of Georgia; MOORE, of Louisiana; PETTUS, of Mississippi; JACKSON, of Missouri; ELLIS, of North Carolina; PICKENS, of South Carolina; HARRIS, of Tennessee; CLARK, of Texas; LETCHER, of Virginia, and others.

CAMPAIGNS, BATTLES, SIEGES, CHARGES, SKIRMISHES, Etc.

By GENERAL ROBERT E. LEE.

Generals ALBERT SIDNEY JOHNSTON, JOSEPH E. JOHNSTON, G. T. BEAUREGARD, BRAXTON BRAGG, SAMUEL COOPER, E. KIRBY SMITH, HOOD, LONGSTREET, STONEWALL JACKSON, POLK, HARDEE, EWELL, A. P. HILL, D. H. HILL, TAYLOR, STEWART, FORREST, HAMPTON, S. D. LEE, EARLY, PEMBERTON, BUCKNER, WHEELER, VAN DORN, SMITH, HUGER, MAGRUDER, PRICE, LORING, LOVELL, CHEATHAM, J. E. B. STUART, PICKETT, BRECKINRIDGE, CLEBURNE, FRENCH, FITZHUGH LEE, McCULLOCH, BUTLER, ROSSER, McLAWS, MORGAN, WALKER, WISE, WRIGHT, CHILTON, ALEXANDER, CHAMBLISS, PILLOW, PENDLETON, EVANS, RIPLEY, TILGHMAN, PIKE, DUNCAN and others.

THE CONFEDERATE STATES NAVY,

FROM ITS FIRST ORGANIZATION TO THE END OF THE WAR. NAVAL ENGAGEMENTS, BLOCKADE RUNNING, OPERATIONS OF CRUISERS, TORPEDO SERVICE, Etc.

By ADMIRAL FRANKLIN BUCHANAN, C. S. N.,

Rear-Admiral RAPHAEL SEMMES, Captains TUCKER, PAGE, CATESBY AP R. JONES, TATNALL, INGRAHAM, LYNCH, JOHNSTON, BRENT, BENNETT, HART, GIFT, ETC.

EDITED BY BEN LA BREE,

Author of "The Pictorial Battles of the Civil War," "History of the Confederate States Navy," "Camp Fires of the Confederacy," Etc.
EDITOR OF THE CONFEDERATE WAR JOURNAL.

THE PRENTICE PRESS
(THE COURIER-JOURNAL JOB PRINTING COMPANY, PUBLISHERS)
LOUISVILLE, KY.
1897.

Amusements, diversions and the arts

An unknown Baltimore artist painted this portrait of young Elizabeth Hamill in about 1859.

Singing and dancing, making music, carving, whittling toys for children, drawing, painting and creating pottery – such amusements and relaxations are the source of much of that large and wonderful body of material generically called "folk art." The term is imprecise, of course, but the implication is correct: the material was made by men and women mostly untrained in any artistic discipline – not unskilled, simply untrained. The distinction is most easily recognizable in paintings. Looking at the little girl's portrait on the preceding page one cannot mistake the lack of sophistication in the modeling of the figure, the delineation of the features and the handling of the fine details of clothing. Yet the painting speaks with a directness and freshness that is thoroughly appealing, and this is the quality one prizes in folk art – a spontaneous and unabashed sense of communication. Other characteristics that frequently come forward are unusual choices of material or forms – the folk artist is unrestrained by convention. Take the piece of scrimshaw below, for example: carved on a sperm whale tooth, it is not only rare for being made by a southerner (most scrimshaw was done by New England whaling men), it is also remarkable in showing a storefront – an eccentric choice of subject matter compared to the usual ships, madonnas, whales, landscapes and nude women. In this case, the oddity has been explained by the Charleston Museum, which owns the piece. The donor was the artist who carved it, a Charleston man who became a whaling captain and whose father ran the business depicted here. Captain Harrison copied the image from a photographic

portrait of his father's shop. Unfortunately, few objects are so well documented. Even if it lasts into the present, folk art usually comes with only a whisper of its origins, or no story at all. In that case, it is the job of the investigator to extrapolate from what is known of the times or places where the pieces were made. Thus, we have been able to identify certain types of work with slaves who frequently served in blacksmith shops of New Orleans, provided a plantation with its homely necessities, or turned to whimsey in extraordinary ceramic objects like the effigy jugs shown on the following page. One of the most sophisticated black craftsmen was Joshua Johnston, a freedman of the early 19th Century who made his living as a portrait painter in Baltimore. The songs of slaves, of course, form an important part of the folk music of the South. It may even be that the distinctive southern instrument, the banjo, is derived from African forerunners. A painting from South Carolina in the Abby Aldrich Rockefeller Folk Art Collection shows a group of slaves dancing to the music played on a gourd fitted with a wooden neck and strings. Could it be a prototype banjo? No one knows. Such are the mysteries that characterize the study and search for folk art. What we are left with finally are the objects themselves — bereft of history, makers' names or place of origin. Though it is frustrating to the scholar, this lack of documentary baggage may enable us to look more closely, without prejudice or distorting information, at the objects themselves — to see them truly for what they are. And this, after all, is what art is all about.

However decorative the everyday work of potters may be, there always seems to be a leftover desire to create something different, and many ceramic workers turn to sculpture on these occasions. The pieces shown here – an array of whimsy that reveals delightful humor – were probably done in off hours, perhaps as gifts for relatives or friends, or for no other reason except fun. *Left:* The lion was bought by a collector from a niece of the potter, John Bell, of a Shenandoah Valley family. The potter's niece said her uncle had made it for her. It is one of three similar lions known. The group of effigy jugs below are believed to have been made late in the 19th Century by slaves and former slaves. The tallest figure, representing a soldier, is said to burlesque a local minister in the area of Greenwood, South Carolina. *Opposite page:* The figure of a seated man may be a portrait of the potter himself, Anthony W. Baecher of Winchester, Virginia. Beside it is a whole scene, rare in pottery, made by two workers at the Eberly Pottery in Strasburg, Virginia, in 1894. It is thought to have commemorated the thirtieth anniversary of a Civil War battle fought at Fisher's Hill, Virginia, in September, 1864.

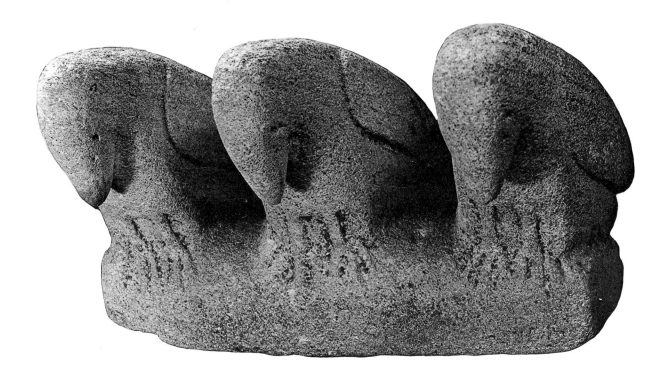

Three winsome, abstract birds, cut from the local limestone of Tennessee, are by a long-lived folk artist, Will Edmondson, who was born in the year the Civil War ended and died in 1950. *Below:* An unknown metal craftsman, probably a blacksmith or a foundry worker, fabricated this wonderfully realistic fish of copper. It was used as a weather vane, perhaps at the fish market in Savannah.

Pierced, or open work, stone grave markers like these are unique to one area of North Carolina. Found in two different churchyards, and bearing dates thirty years apart, they could be by the same artist. Tombstones were sometimes erected long after burial, especially in small communities with no resident stonemason. People would wait to take advantage of the arrival of an itinerant mason to memorialize a long deceased relative. The fact that these two stones, and others like them, are in churchyards not far apart — and are found nowhere else — suggests a local worker.

Three-dimensional folk art has taken many forms – from whittled cane handles to elaborate sculptures. *Upper left:* A jewelry or keepsake box carved from a coconut shell was found in South Carolina and dates before 1825. *Above:* This handsome Indian maiden, about eighteen inches high, was cut from cypress and bears traces of red paint. *Lower left:* This painted wooden mermaid carved of oak disported herself in a garden fountain in Baltimore. *Right:* Here are two canes from Tennessee: the straight-handled one was owned by Joseph Greer, the messenger who brought news of the victory at King's Mountain, Tennessee to the Continental Congress in Philadelphia. *Far right:* Nearly four feet tall, this painted wooden figure of a dancing Negro was carved in Charleston by an unknown artist.

The Oxford English Dictionary devotes several columns to the definition of the word "fiddle," but the best way to understand the fiddle is to hear it played. The distinction between it and the violin lies not only in how it is played but in the music it delivers: when "Turkey in the Straw" comes from a Stradivarius, the violin becomes a fiddle. Although the instruments may appear identical, fiddles are usually more simply and crudely made than violins, because they are often the work of the amateur musicians who play them. As the pasted label on the back of this elegantly-shaped fiddle indicates, the maker was not only the "best jig fiddler in the whole country" but left-handed as well.

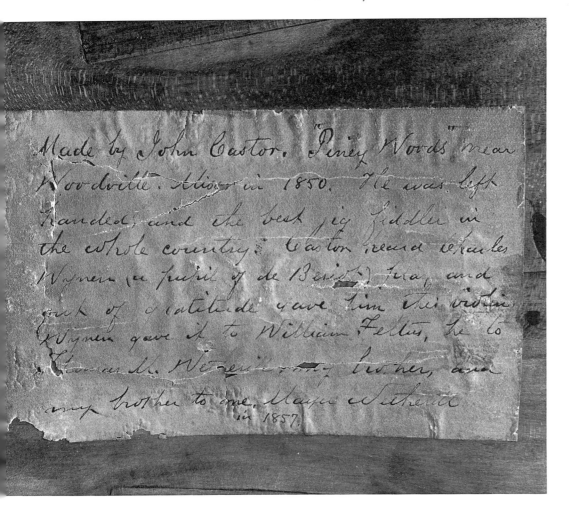

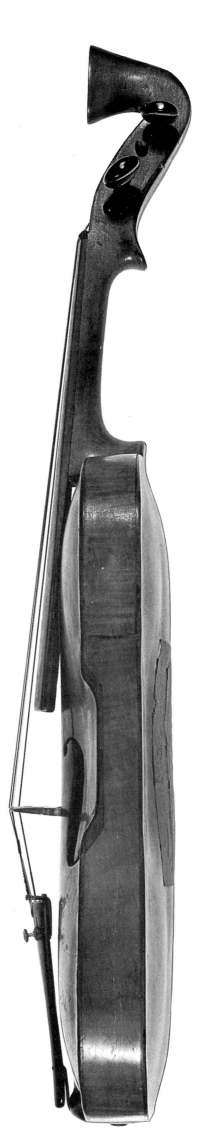

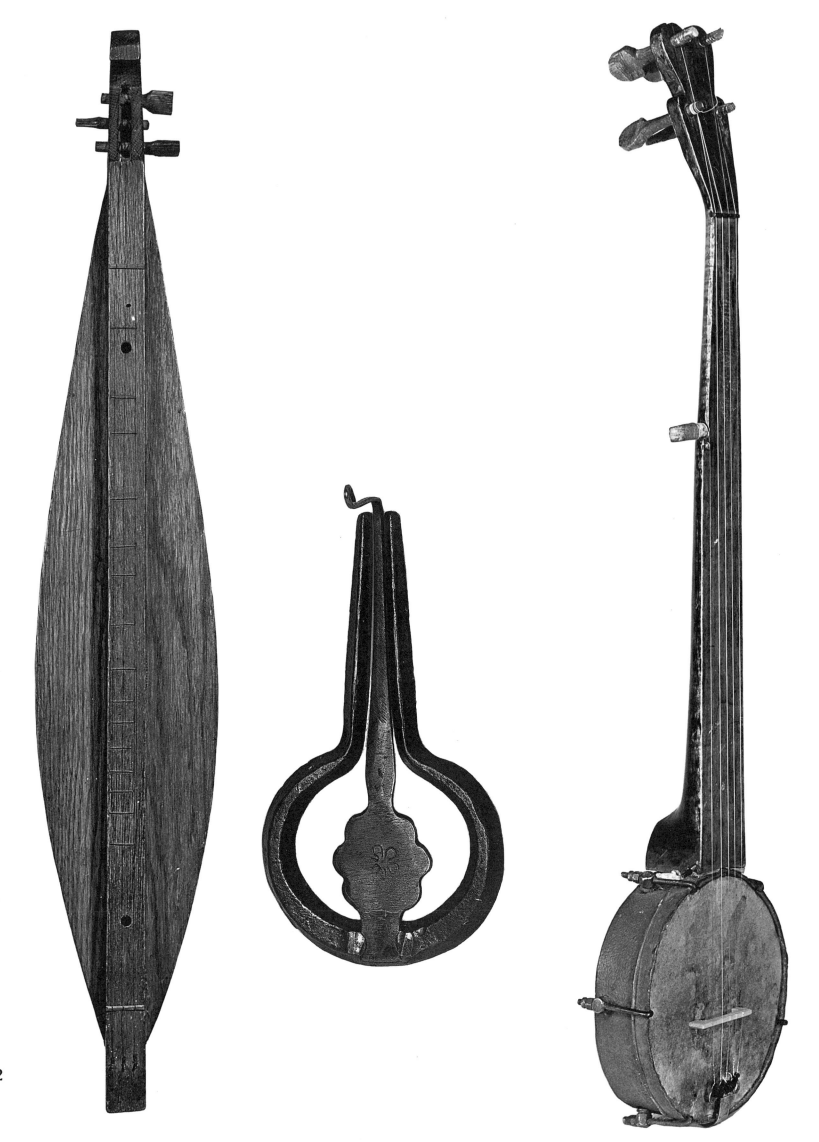

212

The most popular and truly southern folk instruments are the dulcimer and the banjo. The origin of the dulcimer can be traced to Swedish, German, and French antecedents. The banjo may be more truly indigenous to the South, although there are African instruments which suggest an earlier origin. The dulcimers shown are the plucked variety, as opposed to hammered dulcimers. They are held on the player's lap, and one hand moves a short stick up and down the fretboard to change the tone of the melody string while the other hand strums the strings. *Left:* The homemade banjo combines a commercial neck with a hoop of welded wrought iron and carriage bolts. Lending its drone to the sound of the dulcimer and the driving rhythm of the banjo in many folk bands was the Jew's harp, left center, one of the cheapest and easiest of all instruments to play. Millions of them, like the one shown here, were imported from Europe throughout the 19th Century.

214

A special form of calligraphy mixed with drawing is known as "fraktur," from the German word suggesting the angular, fractured quality of the letters. Southern fraktur is most common in Virginia, a heritage of the many immigrants who moved down the wagon road from Pennsylvania in the late 18th and early 19th Centuries. Usually associated with birth and baptismal certificates, fraktur becomes art in the hands of its most skillful practitioners. *Left:* One of the most delightful frakturs is the birth record of George Manger in 1809; it depicts Adam and Eve in the Garden of Eden with a rueful but militant angel at the right. The watercolor and ink drawing contains the details of the child's birth in the heart at the left and a stanza from a hymn at the right. *Below:* This simpler, but no less charming, birth record from North Carolina, may have been executed by a female artist. Some of the floral drawing is similar to that done by students at the Salem Academy. Not fraktur as such, but similar in style, is this small booklet, at right, a birthday ode painted by a Salem artist for Brother Samuel Kramsch, at one time the headmaster of Salem Academy. The booklet is bound in silk-covered cardboard.

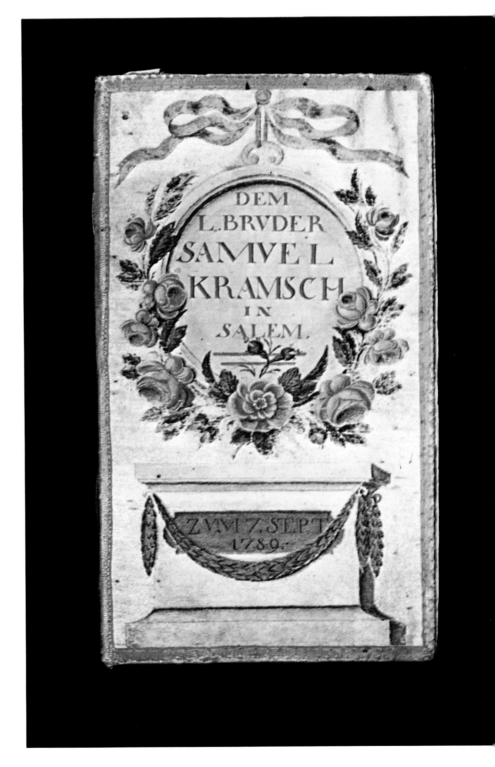

With pen and brush. Drawing, painting, and calligraphy all found a place in the visual arts of the early South. Indeed, drawing was one of the "polite" arts taught to young ladies at such well-run institutions as Salem Academy in North Carolina, originally begun as a Moravian school and opened to the general public in 1802. The group of "keepsakes" at left represent various forms in which the Salem girls demonstrated their abilities — pin cushions, memory books, decorated boxes, needlecases, and a valentine. Somewhat less polite, but full of flavor, is the 1760 drawing below, one of the few firsthand sketches of everyday southern life at this early date. Here are a group of Charleston friends in the Manigault family dining room. The ladies have presumably withdrawn; the cartoon balloons show the men are toasting each other and an unidentified "Carolina," probably a ship bearing their rice or indigo crop to foreign markets. *Left:* Still another degree of skill is shown in this painting. Although not an amateur, the artist was primarily an architect and engineer. He was Marie Adrien Persac, who also made the engraved map from which a piece of Bohemian porcelain took its design (see page 112).

More than a few free black men proved themselves accomplished artists, but none succeeded so well as Joshua Johnston of Baltimore. As early as 1796, he was listed under his trade in the city directory – the first Negro portrait painter in America.

About 1810 Johnston painted this pair of portraits of Mr. and Mrs. Benjamin Yoe of Baltimore with their children. Though the faces seem real enough, Johnston's lack of formal art training is revealed in his stiff handling of the bodies and arms.

Above: The child in the painting may look like a girl, but he is in fact a grandnephew of Thomas Jefferson, dressed in the high fashion of the 1850s. *Right:* Also from an illustrious family are the two brothers in this painting: the elder was named directly for his forebear, the early Virginia governor, Alexander Spotswood. This highly accomplished, yet naive, painting is unusual in depicting a black nurse; oddly, few southern paintings portray the life of slaves. The double portrait is also interesting for its depiction of a boyish sport – hunting birds with bow and arrow. *Far right:* A better armed hunter is shown in a small painting done on velvet, possibly by a student at the Salem Academy in North Carolina.

This painting of an unidentified estate called
the Castle of Montgomery served double
duty; it was used to cover a fireplace opening
in summer. Legend has it that the painter of
the fireboard was an architect who worked
near Woodruff, South Carolina, before 1830.

Left: Few more charming views of country life
exist than this scene of a Virginia plantation,
painted by an anonymous artist about 1825.
With its giant grapes and exaggerated
mountain, the picture is hardly realistic, but it
conveys great love of place.

223

Two southern military men are shown in these paintings: one at the time of his greatest defeat, the other in his moment of victory. *Far right:* General William Darke was an experienced veteran of the French and Indian Wars and several Revolutionary battles. In his mid-fifties, Darke returned to duty to fight the Miami Indians. In the painting's background is a hint of the tragic battle of November 4, 1791 in which Darke's forces were defeated and his youngest son severely wounded. His grim expression reflects the sad history of the event. *Right:* The face of the hero cannot be discerned, but there is no doubt that the artist is portraying Andrew Jackson at the Battle of New Orleans. The scene depicts the British assault on Jackson's entrenchment five miles east of New Orleans, in which the enemy troops were mowed down by artillery and musketry and New Orleans was saved. The painter, Hyacinthe de Laclotte, served as an architect and engineer in the Louisiana army.

Childrens' delights. Before the industrial era, most children's toys were handcarved, whittled, stitched, or nailed by a doting parent, nurse, or uncle. Made simply and quickly for brief amusement and from materials not selected for durability, many have been discarded and lost. Of the number that have survived, little is usually known about their origins. Dolls are easier to identify because they frequently conform to established patterns and are made the same way year after year. Many dolls were imported from Europe and later dressed in new American clothes. The three shown opposite are all certainly southern and handmade: at the right, dressed in blue and white gingham, is a "Maggie/Bessie" doll; the doll at center, from Salem, North Carolina, is dressed as a Moravian sister; and at the left is a "Black Mammy," made over a bottle and wearing a delicate lace cap. Also popular, but fragile, were mechanical toys. One, remaining from about 1900, is the wonderful cigar box pull toy below; as the wheels revolve, the snake's head bobs, the man lifts his arms, and a bell inside the wagon rings – a delightful combination of sight and sound calculated to tickle any toddler. Young children were also recipients of the toys at the left. The crudely carved baby in a cradle is actually a mechanical toy as well; the doll's mouth opens when a peg at the cradle's foot is pulled. Simplest of all toys is the rattle – a wooden box at the end of a handle, here charmingly inlaid with hearts.

Unmistakably a little girl's room, this bedroom from Tennessee dates from the early 19th Century. It is furnished with local curly maple, poplar, and cherry pieces, an appliquéd coverlet and assorted miniature furniture for the dolls. The dolls on the bed are French, those on the child's cane-bottomed chair in the foreground are local. Shown on this page are three toys whose origins are uncertain; they may not have been made in the South (information about such things being very difficult to come by), but in any case, they surely represent the kinds of things that would have amused southern children in the 19th Century. *Above:* The pocket knife was whittled by hand. *Right:* This mouse cage, made of tin and iron, has a little spinning treadmill for the mouse to run inside; certainly for the owner's amusement rather than to exercise the mouse. *Below:* This top is probably a manufactured article because it is so nicely finished; the hole in its side produces a humming sound when the top is spun.

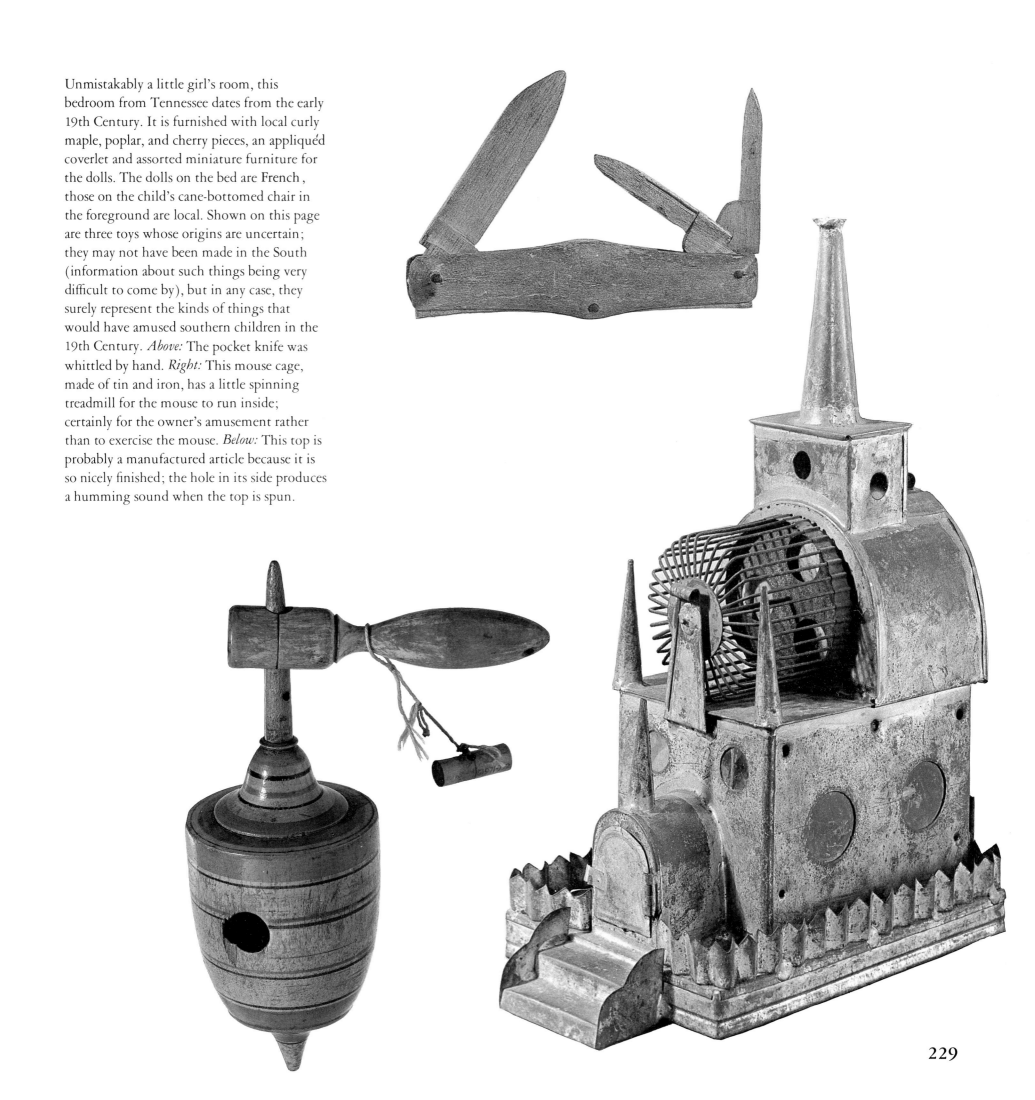

229

The Index of American Design. In a bustling, crowded storeroom behind an exhibition hall at the National Gallery in Washington, D.C., there exists one of the most remarkable archives of the decorative arts to be found anywhere in the world. It is the Index of American Design, a collection of over 17,000 watercolor renderings of the practical, popular, and folk arts of the United States from about 1700 to 1900. The Index was created in 1935 as part of the Federal Art Project of the Works Progress Administration, established to employ out-of-work commercial artists and enable them to maintain their skills during the Depression. Far from "make-work," the project was something curators and scholars had already been lobbying for over a number of years. It met the need for pictorial documentation of America's arts and skills. The artists' efforts were finally halted by the eruption of World War II, but by that time more than three hundred men and women had worked in museums, historical societies, and private collections in thirty-five states. In the South, unfortunately, only Virginia, Kentucky, Louisiana, and Texas were covered in any major way. This was partly because many southern states already had Community Art Centers where local artists were employed as teachers, and also because, then as now, folk material was not well known. Nevertheless, many wonderful objects turned up.

Left: A woolen rag rug made by Shakers. *Above:* A beaver hat box from Virginia.

New Orleans became justly famous for its decorative wrought iron and metal work at a very early date. *Left and right:* Two unusual objects from there are these locksmith's signs, made by a man who was in that business over sixty-four years. *Above:* The fanciful appearance of the wrought iron piece belies its macabre function: it is a slave collar, dating from the 1850s. *Far right:* In Gonzales, Texas, an Index artist preserved the appearance of this weathervane atop the local fire station; its maker is unknown. *Center, opposite page:* The torchlight belonged to a Mississippi volunteer fire company. Made of silvered copper, it was evidently carried in parades.

233

234

Though the objects on these pages look like children's toys, in all probability only the Shaker doll, far right, truly qualifies as such. *Left:* The male figure, with movable hands and feet, is from Arkansas. He is made of ash stained brown and has red toe and fingernails; nothing else is known about him. The curiously cubist pair of chickens has had a colorful, though not necessarily true, history. They are said to have been made by a slave of Jean Lafitte – the French pirate/blacksmith from New Orleans – and presented to the proprietor of the original Absinthe House, a famous drinking establishment still in existence at a different location. *Right:* The mammy figure that looks like a doll comes from Virginia and actually served as a weighted doorstop.

Simple, utilitarian objects captured the eyes of Index artists as readily as sophisticated pieces. *Left:* A hatrack from Texas has carved, wooden supports resembling hooves – an unmistakable mark of its origin. *Below:* This is a charmingly decorated pierced-tin foot warmer from Kentucky; the accompanying story in the Index files relates that in the 1790s similar boxes were carried to church on winter Sundays to warm the feet of women and children. Anyone born before the age of the electric washing machine will recognize the scrub board, though few may have seen one so crudely made of pine and cottonwood twigs. *Opposite page:* A log-cut mortar and pestle (for grinding corn), a partly-mechanized dough mixing box, and an object described in Index files as a coffee grinder. Actually, the wooden wheel and sharply V-shaped trough were probably used for grinding spices, as many similar objects in metal are known to have been used.

237

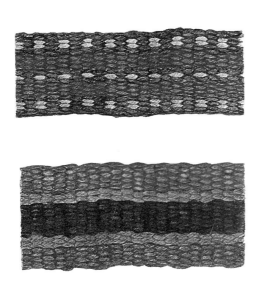

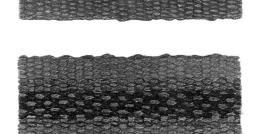

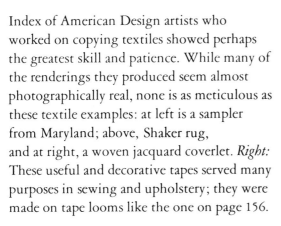

Index of American Design artists who worked on copying textiles showed perhaps the greatest skill and patience. While many of the renderings they produced seem almost photographically real, none is as meticulous as these textile examples: at left is a sampler from Maryland; above, Shaker rug, and at right, a woven jacquard coverlet. *Right:* These useful and decorative tapes served many purposes in sewing and upholstery; they were made on tape looms like the one on page 156.

As has been seen time and again in this book, the American South – every bit as much as the North – was enriched by the yeasty influence of immigrants from many parts of the world. Perhaps in no single object is this so clear as in this figure of "Liberty," carved by an Italian, Eliodoro Parete, who settled in West Virginia sometime after 1863. Both his heritage and his enthusiasm for an adopted country pervade the sculpture, in subject and in its dramatic style. Here is an unabashed proclamation of devotion to the ideal that brought immigrants to these shores, a touching and heroic work.

Another immigrant, Pierre Joseph Landry, from Brittany, became Louisiana's most famous folk sculptor and a major figure in 19th-Century art. His work was not recognized until nearly a century after its creation. Landry served as a captain under Andrew Jackson in the Battle of New Orleans and had carved out a successful career as a planter before a debilitating disease led him to turn to sculpture. His largest surviving work is this "Wheel of Life," depicting the ages of man in nine symbolic episodes. Though quite a few Landry sculptures are known, it remains a challenge to the antique and folk art student to discover others. As we hope this book has shown, the quest is worthy of the effort.

1834

Acknowledgements

For their unstinting assistance and generosity, the author owes a special debt of thanks to Frank Horton, Carolyn Weekley and Brad Rauschenberg of the Museum of Early Southern Decorative Arts, Winston-Salem, North Carolina. Particular appreciation is also due to Graham Hood of Colonial Williamsburg and Paula Welshimer and Frances Griffin of Old Salem.

The following individuals and staffs rendered invaluable aid in gathering photographs and information for this book:

Jay P. Altmayer, Mobile, Alabama;
Association for the Preservation of Virginia Antiquities, Fredericksburg and
    Richmond;
Augusta Richmond County Museum, Augusta, Georgia;
Lupton Avery, Chattanooga, Tennessee;
H. Parrott Bacot, Anglo-American Art Museum, Baton Rouge, Louisiana;
Mrs. Robert Baker, Mrs. Paul Cable, Houston Antique Museum, Chattanooga,
    Tennessee;
William Baker, Tennessee State Museum, Nashville;
Russell Bastedo, Kenmore, Fredericksburg, Virginia;
Joanne Brooks, Redding, Connecticut;
John Burrison, Georgia State University, Atlanta;
J. W. Carpenter, Port Jervis, New York;
James Carter, Donald Herold, Kenneth Jones, The Charleston Museum,
    Charleston, South Carolina;
Judith Wragg Chase, Old Slave Mart Museum, Charleston, South Carolina;
Mr. and Mrs. William T. Cocke III, Sewanee, Tennessee;
Colonial Williamsburg, Audio-Visual Department, Department of Collections,
    Williamsburg, Virginia;
Katherine M. Davis, The National Society of the Colonial Dames, Commonwealth
    of Kentucky, Louisville;
James D. Didier, Louisiana Landmarks Society, New Orleans;
Ernest Dieringer, Redding, Connecticut;
Dale Woods Dingledine, The Baltimore Museum of Art, Baltimore, Maryland;
Thomas Eader, Carroll Mansion, Baltimore, Maryland;
Claudia Eckstein, San Antonio Museum Association, San Antonio, Texas;
Kathleen Ewing, Peggy Blechman, National Gallery of Art, Washington, D.C.;
Letitia Galbraith, National Trust for Historic Preservation, Washington, D.C.;
Wendell Garrett, Rayburn Dobson, *The Magazine ANTIQUES,* New York;
Ann Golavin, Susan Myers, Smithsonian Institution, Washington, D.C.;
Mr. and Mrs. Thomas Goodbrad, Mobile, Alabama;
Henry Green, St. Simon's Island, Georgia;
Mrs. Sumner Greer, Conde-Charlotte House, Mobile, Alabama;
Mrs. Gettys Guille, Rowan Museum and Old Stone House, Salisbury, North
    Carolina;
Jane Hamilton-Merritt, Redding, Connecticut;
Hammond-Harwood House, Annapolis, Maryland;
James Harter, Louisiana State Museum, New Orleans;
Mrs. R. D. Herbert, Jr., Travellers' Rest, Nashville, Tennessee;
Historic Columbus Foundation, Columbus, Georgia;
Samuel C. O. Holt, Washington, D.C.;
Thaddeus G. Holt, Washington, D.C.;
Mary Hubbard, *Antique Monthly,* Tuscaloosa, Alabama;
Mrs. Daniel Huger, Charleston, South Carolina;
Frances and Ross Inglis, Edenton, North Carolina;
Thomas Jefferson Memorial Foundation, Charlottesville, Virginia;
Mary Carter Jones, Redding, Connecticut;

James Kronen, Kronen Gallery, New York;
Bethany Lambdin, Natchez, Mississippi;
Jean Lipman, Cannondale, Connecticut;
Mildred McGehee, Dallas County Heritage Society, Dallas, Texas;
Sarah B. McGehee, Natchez, Mississippi;
Natchez Garden Club, Natchez, Mississippi;
R. E. Neville, Jr., Mobile, Alabama;
New York State Historical Association, Cooperstown, New York;
Vernon Paine, Atlanta Historical Society, Atlanta, Georgia;
Pilgrimage Garden Club, Natchez, Mississippi;
Jessie Poesch, Newcomb College, New Orleans, Louisiana;
Lois Olcott Price, The Filson Club, Louisville, Kentucky;
Priscilla Price, The Corning Museum of Glass, Corning, New York;
Ian Quimby, Arlene Palmer, Karol A. Schmiegel, The Henry Francis du Pont
    Winterthur Museum, Winterthur, Delaware;
Peter M. Rippe, The Harris County Heritage Society, Houston, Texas;
Alicia Rudolf, Historic Charleston Foundation, Charleston, South Carolina;
Beatrix Rumford, Abby Aldrich Rockefeller Folk Art Collection, Williamsburg,
    Virginia;
James B. L. Rush, Winston-Salem, North Carolina;
Dr. and Mrs. Charles Rutherford, Mobile, Alabama;
Albert Sack, Israel Sack, Inc., New York;
Sidney Adair Smith, Mobile, Alabama;
Lina Steele, Index of American Design, National Gallery of Art, Washington, D.C.;
Stone Mountain Memorial Association, Stone Mountain, Georgia;
Stratford Hall Plantation, Robert E. Lee Memorial Association, Stratford, Virginia;
Nancy Sweezy, Jugtown Pottery, Seagrove, North Carolina;
Jack M. Tindel, Mobile, Alabama;
Mrs. Benjamin C. Toledano, New Orleans, Louisiana;
Anna Wadsworth, Georgia Council for the Arts, Atlanta;
Westville Historic Handicrafts, Inc., Lumpkin, Georgia;
Mrs. Forrest Wilson, Historic Mobile Preservation Society, Mobile, Alabama;
William E. Wiltshire III, Richmond, Virginia;
Bill Worthen, Arkansas Territorial Restoration, Little Rock.

242

Bibliography

SOCIAL HISTORY

Boorstin, Daniel. *The Americans: The Colonial Experience.* New York: Random House, 1958.

Bridenbaugh, Carl. *Myths and Realities: Societies of the Colonial South.* New York: Atheneum, 1974.

Cash, W. J. *The Mind of the South.* London: Thames and Hudson Ltd., 1971.

Clark, Thomas D., and Ham, F. Gerald. *Pleasant Hill and Its Shakers.* Pleasant Hill, Ky.: Shakertown Press, 1968.

Cullison, William R. "Gallier House: The Home of a Nineteenth-Century New Orleans Architect." *The Magazine ANTIQUES,* Volume CII Number 3, September, 1972.

Dowdey, Clifford. *The Great Plantation.* Charles City, Va.: Berkeley Plantation, 1958.

Fleischmann, C. L. *Trade, Manufacture and Commerce in the United States of America.* Jerusalem: Israel Program for Scientific Translations, Ltd., 1970.

Griffin, Frances. *Old Salem: An Adventure in Historic Preservation.* Winston-Salem, N.C.: Old Salem, Inc., 1970.

————————. *Old Salem in Pictures.* Charlotte, N.C.: McNally and Loftin Publishers, 1972.

Noël Hume, Ivor. *A Guide to Artifacts of Colonial America.* New York: Alfred A. Knopf, Inc., 1969.

————————. *Five Artifact Studies.* Williamsburg, Va.: Colonial Williamsburg Foundation, 1973.

Osborne, John, and editors of Time-Life Books. *The Old South.* New York: Time-Life Books, 1968.

Ring, Betty. "Salem Female Academy." *The Magazine ANTIQUES,* Volume CVI Number 3, September, 1974.

Rippe, Peter M. "Harris County Heritage Society of Houston." *The Magazine ANTIQUES,* Volume CVIII Number 3, September, 1975.

Spruill, Julia Cherry. *Women's Life and Work in the Southern Colonies.* New York: W. W. Norton & Co., Inc., 1972.

Sweeny, John A. H. *Winterthur Illustrated.* Winterthur, Del.: A Winterthur Book, 1971.

Taylor, Lonn. "The McGregor-Grimm House at Winedale, Texas." *The Magazine ANTIQUES,* Volume CVIII Number 3, September, 1975.

Tharin, W. C. *A Directory of Marengo County for 1860-61.* Demopolis, Ala.: The Marengo County Historical Society, 1973.

The Journal and Letters of Philip Vickers Fithian. Williamsburg, Va.: Colonial Williamsburg, 1965.

Williams, T. Harry, and editors of *Life. The Life History of the United States,* Volume 5, *The Union Sundered, 1849-1865.* New York: Time, Inc., 1963.

GENERAL ANTIQUES

Arts in Virginia. Volume Two, Winter, 1962.

Classical America 1815-1845. Newark, N.J.: The Newark Museum, 1963.

Comstock, Helen. *The Concise Encyclopedia of American Antiques.* New York: Hawthorn Books, 1965.

Drepperd, Carl W. *A Dictionary of American Antiques.* New York: Award Books, 1970.

Garrett, Wendell; ed. *Antiques In Kentucky.* Reprinted from *The Magazine ANTIQUES,* March and April, 1974.

Miller, Robert W. *The Fabulous Houston.* Des Moines: Wallace-Homestead Book Co., 1971.

Winchester, Alice; ed. *The Museum of Early Southern Decorative Arts.* Reprinted from *The Magazine ANTIQUES,* January, 1967.

Ormsbee, Thomas H. *Know Your Heirlooms.* New York: The McBride Company, Inc., 1957.

Savage, George. *Dictionary of Antiques.* New York: Praeger Publishers, Inc., 1970.

Stitt, Susan. *Museum of Early Southern Decorative Arts.* Winston-Salem, N.C.: Old Salem, Inc., 1970.

Wilson, Jose, and Leaman, Arthur. *Decorating Defined.* New York: Simon and Schuster, Inc., 1970.

FURNITURE

Baltimore Furniture: The Work of Baltimore and Annapolis Cabinetmakers from 1760 to 1810. Baltimore, Md.: The Baltimore Museum of Art, 1947.

Battison, Edwin A. and Kane, Patricia E. *The American Clock 1725-1865.* Greenwich, Conn.: New York Graphic Society Ltd., 1973.

Beirne, Rosamond Randall. "John Shaw, Cabinetmaker." *The Magazine ANTIQUES,* Volume LXXVIII Number 6, December, 1960.

Bivins, John, Jr. "A Piedmont North Carolina Cabinetmaker." *The Magazine ANTIQUES,* Volume CIII Number 5, May, 1973.

Bridenbaugh, Carl. *The Colonial Craftsman.* Chicago and London: The University of Chicago Press, 1974.

Burton, E. Milby. *Charleston Furniture 1700-1825.* Columbia: University of South Carolina Press, 1955.

Chippendale, Thomas. *The Gentleman and Cabinet-Maker's Director.* Reprint. New York: Dover Publications, Inc., 1966.

Downs, Joseph. *American Furniture – Queen Anne and Chippendale Periods.* New York: The Macmillan Company, 1962.

Dunstan, William Edward III. "The Colonial Cabinetmaker in Tidewater Virginia." *Virginia Cavalcade.* Volume XX Number 1, Summer, 1970.

Elder, William Voss III. *Baltimore Painted Furniture 1800-1840.* Baltimore, Md.: The Baltimore Museum of Art, 1972.

Fales, Dean A., Jr., and Bishop, Robert. *American Painted Furniture 1660-1880.* New York: E. P. Dutton & Co., Inc., 1972.

Gusler, Wallace B., and Gill, Harold B., Jr. "Some Virginia Chairs; A Preliminary Study." *The Magazine ANTIQUES,* Volume CI Number 4, April, 1972.

Horton, Frank L. "The Work of an Anonymous Carolina Cabinetmaker." *The Magazine ANTIQUES,* Volume CI Number 1, January, 1972.

Horton, Frank L., and Weekley, Carolyn J. *The Swisegood School of Cabinetmaking.* Winston-Salem, N.C.: Museum of Early Southern Decorative Arts, 1973.

Kentucky Furniture. Louisville, Ky.: The J. B. Speed Art Museum, 1974.

Maryland Queen Anne and Chippendale Furniture of the Eighteenth Century. Baltimore, Md.: The Baltimore Museum of Art, 1968.

McClinton, Mary Clay. "Robert Wilson, Kentucky Cabinetmaker." *The Magazine ANTIQUES,* Volume CIII Number 5, May, 1973.

Montgomery, Charles F. *American Furniture, The Federal Period 1788-1825.* New York: The Viking Press, 1966.

Nineteenth Century America, Furniture and Other Decorative Arts. New York: The Metropolitan Museum of Art, 1970.

Poesch, Jessie J. *Early Furniture of Louisiana 1750-1830.* New Orleans: Louisiana State Museum, 1972.

Sheraton, Thomas. *Cabinet-Maker and Upholster's Drawing Book.* New York: Dover Publications, Inc., 1972.

Steinfeldt, Cecilia, and Stover, Donald Lewis. *Early Texas Furniture and Decorative Arts.* San Antonio: Trinity University Press, 1973.

The Williamsburg Collection of Antique Furnishings. Williamsburg, Va.: Colonial Williamsburg Foundation, 1973.

Weekley, Carolyn. "James Gheen, Piedmont North Carolina Cabinetmaker." *The Magazine ANTIQUES,* Volume CIII Number 5, May, 1973.

Winchester, Alice, and the staff of *The Magazine ANTIQUES. The Antiques Treasury of Furniture and Other Decorative Arts.* New York: Galahad Books, 1959.

————————, "Furniture of the Old South 1640-1820." *The Magazine ANTIQUES,* Volume LXI Number 1, January, 1952.

SILVER AND METALWORK

Bacot, H. Parrot, and Lambdin, Bethany B. "Nineteenth-Century Silver in Natchez." *The Magazine ANTIQUES,* Volume XCIX Number 3, March, 1971.

Bridwell, Margaret M. "Three Early Kentucky Silversmiths." *The Magazine ANTIQUES,* Volume LXXVIII Number 6, December, 1960.

Caldwell, Benjamin H., Jr. "Tennessee Silversmiths." *The Magazine ANTIQUES,* Volume C Number 3, September, 1971.

Capron, John D. "Virginia Iron Furnaces of the Confederacy." *Virginia Cavalcade,* Volume XVII Number 2, Autumn, 1967.

Christian, Marcus. *Negro Ironworkers of Louisiana, 1718-1900.* Gretna: Pelican Publishing Company, 1972.

Farnham, Katharine Gross, and Efird, Callie Huger. "Early Silversmiths and the Silver Trade in Georgia." *The Magazine ANTIQUES,* Volume XCIX Number 3, March, 1971.

Hood, Graham. *American Silver, A History of Style 1650-1900.* New York: Praeger Publishers, Inc., 1971.

Maryland Silver. Baltimore, Md.: The Baltimore Museum of Art, 1975.

Montgomery, Charles F. *A History of American Pewter.* New York: Praeger Publishers, Inc., 1973.

Nineteenth Century Natchez-Made Silver. Baton Rouge: Louisiana State University, 1970.

Smith, Sidney Adair. "Mobile Silversmiths and Jewelers 1820-1867." *The Magazine ANTIQUES,* Volume XCIX Number 3, March, 1971.

Southern Furniture and Silver. Baton Rouge: Louisiana State University, 1968.

Southern Silver. Houston, Tex.: The Museum of Fine Arts, 1968.

Warren, David B. "Southern Silver." *The Magazine ANTIQUES,* Volume XCIX Number 3, March, 1971.

GLASS

Amelung Glass. Baltimore, Md.: The Maryland Historical Society, 1952.

McKearin, Helen, and McKearin, George S. *Two Hundred Years of American Blown Glass.* New York: Bonanza Books, 1950.

Papert, Emma. *The Illustrated Guide to American Glass.* New York: Hawthorn Books, 1972.

CERAMICS

Bivins, John, Jr., *The Moravian Potters in North Carolina.* Chapel Hill: University of North Carolina Press, 1972.

Blasberg, Robert W. *George E. Ohr and His Biloxi Pottery.* Port Jervis, N.Y.: J. W. Carpenter, 1973.

Larsen, Ellovise Baker. *American Historical Views on Staffordshire China.* New York: Dover Publications, Inc., 1975.

Wiltshire, William E. III. *Folk Pottery of the Shenandoah Valley.* New York: E. P. Dutton & Co., Inc., 1975.

FOLK ART

Black, Mary, and Lipman, Jean. *American Folk Painting.* New York: Bramhall House, 1966.

Chase, Judith Wragg. *Afro-American Art & Craft.* New York: Van Nostrand Reinhold Company, 1971.

Folk Art in America: A Living Tradition. Atlanta: The High Museum, 1974.

Hornung, Clarence P. *Treasury of American Design.* Volumes I and II. New York: Harry N. Abrams, Inc., 1972.

Journal of Early Southern Decorative Arts, Volume I Number 2. Winston-Salem, N.C.: Museum of Early Southern Decorative Arts, November, 1975.

——————— , Volume II Number 1. Winston-Salem, N.C.: Museum of Early Southern Decorative Arts, May, 1976.

Lipman, Jean. *American Folk Art in Wood, Metal and Stone.* New York: Pantheon Books, 1948.

——————— , and Winchester, Alice. *The Flowering of American Folk Art 1776-1876.* New York: The Viking Press, Inc., 1974.

Louisiana Folk Art. Baton Rouge: Louisiana State University, 1972.

Montgomery, Charles F., and Kane, Patricia E. *American Art 1750-1800 Towards Independence.* Boston: New York Graphic Society Ltd., 1976.

Simmons, Linda Crocker. *Jacob Frymire: American Limner.* Washington, D.C.: Corcoran Gallery of Art, 1975.

Wust, Klaus. *Folk Art in Stone: Southwest Virginia.* Edinburg, Va.: Shenandoah History, 1970.

——————— . *Virginia Fraktur: Penmanship as Folk Art.* Edinburg: Shenandoah History, 1972.

TEXTILES

Harbeson, Georgiana Brown. *American Needlework.* New York: Coward-McCann, Inc., Bonanza Books, 1938.

Orlofsky, Patsy, and Orlofsky, Myron. *Quilts in America.* New York: McGraw-Hill, Inc., 1974.

Pforr, Effie Chambers. *Award Winning Quilts.* Birmingham: Oxmoor House, Inc., 1974.

Stafford, Carleton L., and Bishop, Robert. *America's Quilts and Coverlets.* New York: Weathervane Books, 1974.

GUNS

Lindsay, Merrill. *One Hundred Great Guns.* New York: Walker and Company, 1967.

——————— . *The Kentucky Rifle.* The Historical Society of York County. New York: Arma Press, 1972.

Peterson, Harold L. *The Fuller Collection of American Firearms.* Chattanooga: Eastern National Park and Monument Association, in Cooperation with Chickamauga and Chattanooga National Military Park, National Park Service, 1967.

TOYS AND DOLLS

McClinton, Katharine Morrison. *Antiques of American Childhood.* New York: Bramhall House, 1970.

O'Brien, Marian Maeve. *The Collector's Guide to Dollhouses and Dollhouse Miniatures.* New York: Hawthorn Books, 1974.

COMMERCIAL AND ADVERTISING

Dietz, Lawrence. *Soda Pop.* New York: Simon and Schuster, Inc., 1973.

Robert, Joseph C. *The Story of Tobacco in America.* Chapel Hill: University of North Carolina Press, 1967.

Catalog of illustrations

246

SOUTHERN ANTIQUES & FOLK ART

Reproduction of objects and manufacture supervised
by Harry H. Lerner of Triton Press, Inc., New York City

Designed by Ladislav Svatos, Easton, Connecticut

Text composed in Fototronic Garamond
by Typographic Art, Inc., Hamden, Connecticut

Color separation photography and film prepared
by Offset Separations Corporation, New York City

Printed by Meehan-Tooker, a division of John Blair & Company,
East Rutherford, New Jersey

Bound by A. Horowitz & Son • Bookbinders, Fairfield, New Jersey

Text sheets are Lustro Offset Enamel Dull
by S. D. Warren Company, a division of Scott Paper Company,
Boston, Massachusetts

Endleaves are Curtis Stoneridge by Lindenmeyr Paper Corporation,
Long Island City, New York

Cover cloth is Sailcloth by The Holliston Mills, Inc.,
Lincoln, Rhode Island

This is number

31808

of the First Edition of 60,000 copies